In Celebration of the 125th Anniversary of the Claremont Opera House

A LIVING HISTORY, RETOLD

Annalisa Parent

Copyright 2022 Claremont Opera House, Inc.

All rights reserved. No part of this publication may be reproduced, distributed, or transmitted in any form or by any means, including photocopying, recording, or other electronic or mechanical methods, without the prior written permission of the publisher, except in the case of brief quotations embodied in critical reviews and certain other noncommercial uses permitted by copyright law. For permission requests, write to the publisher, addressed "Attention: Permissions Coordinator," at the address below.

Laurel Elite Books
P.O. Box 815
Claremont, NH 03743

Ordering Information:
Quantity sales. Special discounts are available on quantity purchases by corporations, associations, and others. For details, contact the publisher at the address above.

Orders by U.S. trade bookstores and wholesalers. Please contact Laurel Elite Books: Tel: (603) 722-0422 or visit www.laurelelite.com.

Printed in the United States of America

Cover Photo By David Putnam

Publisher's Cataloging-in-Publication data
Parent, Annalisa

Stage Whispers: A Living History, Retold
ISBN 978-1-7360587-2-5
Library of Congress Control Number 2022910842

First Edition

Contents

Introduction   v
Introduction to voices   viii

I: An Opera House: How it Came to Be
An Opera House: How it Came to Be   3
The Historical Significance of the Claremont Opera House   5

II. Claremont Town Hall
A Sight to Behold   21
SPOTLIGHT: *Claremont: A Center of Sports Activity*   32

III. The Opera House's Heyday 1910-1930
The Opera House's Heyday 1910-1930   45
Ten Cent Shows?   59
SPOTLIGHT: *Claremont Public School in the Early 20th Century*   64
How High School Graduation Changed the Opera House   73

IV: Movies and Theaters in Claremont: A City on the Cutting Edge

Early Days of Movies in Claremont	83
Movie Theaters' Impact on the Opera House	101

V. The Changing Scene of Music and Dance

Pine Grove Park	107
Music Around Town; Music at The Opera House	115
SPOTLIGHT: *Jazz, Swing and the Big Bands from New Orleans to Pine Grove Park and Roseland*	121
ROSELAND: A New Type of Music; a New Venue	133
SPOTLIGHT: *Band Music in Claremont*	139
SPOTLIGHT: *Buster Keating Local Music Celebrity*	146

VII. Other Entertainments and Local Parks

Other Entertainments and Local Parks	159

VIII. The End of The Opera House?

Another Big Shift in Entertainment Pushed the Opera House into Near Obscurity	167
A Second Wind	171

IX. Claremont's Cultural Future

Claremont's Cultural Future	179
Afterword	183

Works Cited	187
Board President's Acknowledgements	191
Author's Note	195
Author's Acknowledgments	197
About the Author	199
Sponsorships	201

Introduction

A century ago, Claremont was a cultural mecca—a destination which drew performers from as far off as Boston and Montreal—and spectators from everywhere in between.

Imagine if the popular bands of today were to make Claremont a tour stop, if your favorite A-list actors stopped by the local cinema for an appearance, or your favorite sports stars played right here in town.

So it was for a period of time right here in our fair city.

The Claremont Opera House was a huge draw to big names, to be sure, but other venues in Claremont drew celebrities as well. A few of these places exist today, in altered form, and many of them are gone. None of these venues stand as tall, as proud, and as well preserved as the Claremont Opera House.

The history of the Opera House has not been without controversy, from its conceptualization when Claremont residents disputed the merits of an opera house over a city sewer system, to the 1960s debate on whether to tear the building down or preserve it.

Even today, the Opera House is often misunderstood, its very name something of a misnomer. For a venue with "opera" in the title, it has, in fact, staged very few opera performances over its 125-year history. Its programming has been far more varied, with performers coming from all over the world, and right here in town; with performances from the scripted, scored, and professional to the showcase of local dance schools.

Stage Whispers: A Living History, Retold traces the shifting tides of entertainment in Claremont, demonstrating how each of the venues played a role in drawing quality entertainment to the city. Its focus is not a comprehensive view of all arts and entertainment from 1897 to 1980, but rather one which highlights the arts and entertainment experience during that time period through the voices of area residents. These narratives are drawn from *Claremont, New Hampshire - A Living History*, a 1980 oral history project featuring forty-one interviews with fifty-one citizens.

The original oral history was funded by a $19,000 grant from the New Hampshire Council for the Humanities and sponsored by the City of Claremont.

The interviews were performed by historian Gerald Gatz "to spark a discussion which could lead, among other things, to an awareness for the city's unique history and a heightened individual awareness of state-of-the-art Claremont." (Croft 9)

Though the audio recordings are now decades old, they preserve important moments in our history—the inception of the Claremont Opera House, the heyday of big band music, and the changes that came with modern inventions we daily take for granted: talking movies, the automobile, television, and the interstate, to name a few.

Throughout the retracing of the history of arts and entertainment in Claremont, you will hear voices of its past residents from these recordings. The purpose of this narrative is to highlight the primary source material of residents' voices, to see major artistic movements' impact through the eyes of Claremont residents, and to allow the story to be told from their point of view.

Gift of oral history

By BERTHA EMOND

CLAREMONT, N.H. — The results of the Oral History Project, indexes and tapes, were presented to the Fiske Free Library Tuesday night in the presence of many of the 51 people interviewed by Project Director Gerald Gatz.

Illustrating the theory that pictures speak louder than words, viewers responded to the slides with recollections and identifications, often to the neglect of the accompanying words.

It's a production which will bear viewing again and again, adding details which cannot be grasped at the first time through. It will be shown again Thursday at the meeting of the Claremont Historical Society Museum, 26 Mulberry St., 8 p.m.

Professor Jere Daniell, chairman of the Dartmouth College History Department, introduced the program, as the "academic humanist" required to obtain funding for the project.

Noting that the tapes would probably get more public usage than in any project I've worked on, because of its copious index, Daniell observed they covered the city in its heyday — from 1910-1930. In terms of its past, problems began in the 1920s, when the mills folded.

By 1920, Claremont had almost half the county population, he said, comparing population figures from 1840 to 1920. In 1840 Cornish and Unity had about double their present number of residents.

Refreshments of coffee and cookies were available at the close of the program.

A GIFT — A presentation of the Oral History of Claremont tapes and indexes was made at a special gathering Tuesday night. Accepting the gift from Project Director Gerald Gatz is Marilyn Nagy, research specialist at the Fiske Free Library. (Bertha Emond Photo)

Eagle-Times 10/22/80

A Gift—A presentation of the Oral History of Claremont tapes and indexes was made at a special gathering Tuesday night. Accepting the gift from Project Director Gerald Gatz is Marilyn Nagy, research specialist at the Fiske Free Library. (Bertha Emond Photo, *Eagle Times*, 22 Oct. 1980)

Like the original source materials *Stage Whispers: A Living History, Retold* was made possible through a Community Project Grant from New Hampshire Humanities. Production of the book was sponsored by Claremont Savings Bank.

Introduction to voices

Elizabeth Bell (1885-1989) worked for thirty-five years at the International Shoe Company and retired as an inspector. She was a charter member of Court Virgil H. Barber No. 892 of Catholic Daughters of America, and a communicant of St. Mary Parish.

Earl Bourdon (1917-1993) was a voice for social justice and equality (Clifton-Waite 1) in the Claremont community. He graduated in 1935 from Stevens High School, and later from Suffolk Law School. He also received an honorary doctorate degree in human services from New Hampshire College.

Frank Bush (1902-1996) was a local musician and teacher. In his narrative he talks extensively about music history, but also digs into source material he had collected over the years to share the history of entertainment venues throughout the city.

Charles Chandler (1906-1995) was a lifelong resident of Claremont. Chandler graduated from Stevens High School in 1924. He was a draftsman and tool designer at Jones and Lamson in Springfield, VT for thirty-five years.

Mable Cutting (1910-1998) served in the New Hampshire House of Representatives and on the Claremont School Board where she advocated for students, and especially for equal representation for girls on school athletic teams. She graduated from Stevens High School in 1927.

Bertha Emond (1916-1991) resided in Claremont most of her life. She graduated from St. Mary High School in 1935. From 1975-1985 she was a reporter and photographer for *The Eagle Times* and wrote two regular columns.

Albert D. Leahy Sr. (1903-1994) was a longtime Claremont resident and lawyer. He was appointed a judge and, from 1935 to 1972, he presided over what is now called the Claremont District Court. He served as a New Hampshire Representative to the House from 1931 to 1935.

Paul Mason (1897-1989) resided in Claremont for most of his life. He was a well-known tenor soloist in the area, singing in many choral groups and churches. He also sang in many oratorios and light operas in New Hampshire and Vermont.

Cynthia McKee (1915-1994) was a lifelong Claremont resident who served as both secretary to School District Superintendent of Schools and as City Editor for *The Daily Eagle*, now known as *The Eagle Times*. She served two terms in the New Hampshire House of Representatives.

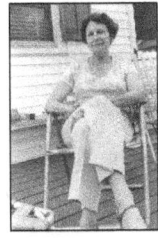

Effie White (1890-1992) was a Claremont resident from 1901 until her death. White spent eight years as music director at Perkins Institute for the blind. She gave piano lessons for over fifty years and was organist and choir director at several local churches.

Other featured Claremont residents:
Arthur Garneau
Laurina Issoire
Alice Joyal
Mildred LaPanne

To hear their own words: https://www.claremontnh.com/historic-resources

> It was bright and sunny when I visited Ms. Issoire at the Marion Phillips Apartments on Broad Street that day. She was sitting in a lawn chair out front working on one of her pen and ink sketches of buildings important to her from her past. It wasn't our first visit together so we greeted each other and started chatting. She knew my oral history project and seemed always eager to talk about her memories of Claremont when she was younger. Besides being beautiful and well executed, her drawings captured a Claremont long gone.
> Gerald Gatz, Project Manager

STAGE WHISPERS | **xi**

Drawings by L. M. Issoire, 1980:
Top left: North St and Broad St Meets. Washington St early 1900s.
Top right: Broad St Bridge, Looking South as remembered from earliest 1900.
Bottom: The Monadnock Mill Block, 1900. Lincoln St.

I: An Opera House: How it Came to Be

An Opera House:
How it Came to Be

For many Claremont residents and visitors, the Claremont Opera House is such an integral city fixture, it seems to have always been here. It is likely few residents question its presence or how it came to be.

After further consideration, of course, one realizes that, though perhaps taken for granted, certainly the Opera House was not always as it is today. So, how did this majestic meeting place and entertainment venue find its place in the heart of Claremont?

Frank Bush, in his review of historical documents, discussed the need for a central community gathering space, and how that building changed over time:

> *The Claremont Opera House: What it Was in the Past, What it Could Be in the Future.* This was a headline in the local media in February of 1977.
>
> In 1783, Ichabod Hitchcock, the only master carpenter in town procured the timber and under his supervision, the congregational meeting house was

built on the highway, near the WHH Moody horse training park.

That was in the vicinity of the present Maple Avenue School. Around the year of 1790, the building was taken down and removed to the village in the location of the present city hall. Then in 1835, the Congregationalist Society moved out of the building to its newly completed meeting house on Pleasant Street.

So, in 1867, pursuant to a vote of the town, the original old town hall was repaired, remodeled, and a new tower was added, all at the cost of $10,000.

March 12, 1895, after nearly two hours of highly contested debate, the aggressive party was victorious in favor of a new town hall. However, two more meetings were needed in order to get an affirmative vote for a $50,000 appropriation. On June 5th, the old hall was sold to Frank P. Maynard for $110, and to everyone's surprise, demolition began two days later.

On July 13, 1895, after another heated discussion that started around the bandstand (because the town hall was now gone), the voters refused the plans submitted by Professor Warren of Boston. He then threatened to sue, and the town paid the architect $1,254.79 for plans that were never used.

Finally, after accepting the plans drawn up by the New York firm of Lamb and Rich, the contract was awarded to Hira Beckwith, the lowest bidder, and work was underway on October 30, 1895.

The Historical Significance of the Claremont Opera House

Claremont has many fine historical treasures, many of which have the honor of appearing on the National Register of Historic Places. In 1973, the Claremont Opera House received the prestigious listing.

> The National Register of Historic Places is the official list of the nation's historic places worthy of preservation. The National Park Service's National Register of Historic Places is part of a national program to coordinate and support public and private efforts to identify, evaluate, and protect America's historic and archeological resources. (National Parks Service)

One of the many reasons the Claremont Opera House was selected for this honor is its architectural significance. The building is one of the best examples in New Hampshire of the Renaissance Revival style, a style of architecture more typically found in larger urban centers than Claremont, and all the more unusual for its location in a rural, industrial community.

According to then-commissioner of the New Hampshire Department of Resources and Economic Development, George Gilman, who submitted the listing application:

> [T]he choice of a sophisticated design by a New York architect for its seat of government, and center of community activities, reflected Claremont's economic, social and political ambitions at the end of the 19th century, and its aspirations to transform itself from a small industrial city to a regional service and cultural center. (1973)

The Claremont Opera House is situated on the southeast corner of Opera House Square, center of the city's business district, on a plot with an 82-foot frontage and 185-foot depth.

The brownstone and brick rectangular building stands two stories in height with a square clock tower extending off-center on the south side and a low hip roof.

Except for the south entrance (which was bricked) and the west entrance with glass doors (the result of converting the first-floor ballroom into city offices and council chamber in 1960), the exterior of the building today is, for the most part, as it was in 1897, including the New Hampshire Coat of Arms over the south-side entrance.

Construction began on October 30, 1895, and the building was dedicated June 22, 1897.

Its architect was Charles A. Rich, of Lamb & Rich, New York City. A native of Beverly, Massachusetts, he graduated from Dartmouth College in 1875 and became professionally associated with Hugh Lamb after studying architecture and spending 1879-1880 in Europe.

A noted architectural firm, Lamb & Rich designed numerous apartments and residences in New York City, college buildings, and Sagamore Hill (Oyster Bay, New York, home of President Theodore Roosevelt), and other opera houses including the East Orange, New Jersey Opera House.

The contractor, Hira Beckwith of Claremont, erected a number of other public buildings in the area, and built many impressive homes in Claremont. Although he was foremost a contractor, he had attended the Asher Benjamin School of Design to study architecture in Windsor, Vermont.

An article on the Opera House's dedication lauded Beckwith's work on the building:

> But [City Hall] is built upon honor, and if Hira R. Beckwith was not accorded the planning, his superintendency of the erection of the building, has resulted in a monument to his skill that should endure for generations. He has made it the work of his life, thus far, and the citizens of Claremont should indeed feel grateful for the faithful, tireless care with which he has watched the structure grow from foundation to tower. It would have been a graceful and creditable act on the part of the building committee, if a public acknowledgment of Mr. Beckwith's faithful administration had entered into the dedicatory programme. (*The National Eagle* 1897)

Most of the Opera House's interior finishings were furnished by Freeman and O'Neil of Claremont.

> **New Public Building at a Glance**
>
> **Style:** Italian Renaissance Revival.
> **Architect:** Charles A. Rich, a native of Beverly, Massachusetts, and graduate of Dartmouth College.
> **Contractor:** Hira Beckwith, an architect in Claremont
> **Foundation:** Green Mountain Rock
> **Base:** Connecticut River Brownstone from Springfield, Massachusetts.
> **Exterior:** nearly one million Lebanon bricks.
> **Inside the Theater:** The theater has a frescoed ceiling and a decorative wall frieze culminating with a proscenium arch adorned with a combination of basswood, painted cream, and a gold leafed molded plaster-work in high relief. Above the proscenium arch there is a circular multicolored fresco of the New Hampshire state seal by Schupboch and Zeller, Boston.
> **Capacity:** The auditorium has a total seating capacity of 783.

Construction of the Opera House began October 30, 1895. *The National Eagle* reported:

> On Monday October 28th, the building committee signed a contract with Mr. [Hira] Beckwith. On account of some changes the exact contract price was $48,619, and the time limit set for completion was February 1, 1897. Active work commenced on the site Wednesday morning, October 30, 1895. Since then, with the exception of a few weeks in the winter of '95, work has progressed without interruption.
>
> The first use made of the lower hall was for a March meeting, in 1897, and on May 8th, Mr. Beckwith, to satisfy a general desire, threw open the building for

public inspection. With that exception it has been closed to the sight-seers for many months.

Because so few residents had been afforded an opportunity to peek inside the new building, and because of the number of visiting dignitaries, the dedication of the building was a significant event for Claremont residents of the day.

People came from far afield hitching their horses into teams to draw their carriages and carts into town. The local newspaper reported that the governor himself arrived in an open carriage pulled by a team of four horses, or a four-in-hand.

Claremont resident Elizabeth Bell was about twelve years old on the day of the dedication ceremony and remembered:

> I remember the day the Opera House was dedicated. My mother and I, we walked up the street and we went to the Opera House to see it.
>
> The governor was here; it was a big day. They had exercises in the afternoon.

Frank Bush shared information from his extensive document collection, highlighting an article in *The Claremont Advocate*, one of the city's two newspapers at the time. *The Claremont Advocate* published news from 1881-1941 and was affectionately known as *"The Advocate."*

> On June 23, 1897, the dedication issue of *The Advocate* devotes the whole front page to perhaps Claremont's biggest event up to this time. The governor and other dignitaries from two states came by special railroad trains. The auditorium held 980 people, but *The*

National Eagle reported that a total of 1,800 were seated and were standing in the aisles and stairways.

The Mediterranean styling was beautifully done by imported artists of the time. The cost of the building was under $70,000. And this was met by selling bonds to Claremont residents.

Along with the usual speeches was a fine musical program. Eastman's Orchestra from Manchester opened with Weber's *Overture to Oberon*. Professor Kramer then presented the Claremont Choral Society with *The Heavens Are Telling* from Haydn's Creation.

There were some critics. Dr. Osmon Way, who was a speaker at the dedication ceremonies said, and we quote, "I was in favor of preserving the older building. Its destruction was to me like an act of vandalism."

He also criticized the placement of the eagle, poor bird! What a low perch for the proud eagle. He should be above the roof where he could bask in the morning sun and flap his wings in the evening breezes.

However, at the end of his dedication speech, he said, and we quote, "as time passes, everyone will have increased pride in the noble structure of which there is no finer in any town in New Hampshire."

The original eagle on its outdoor perch.
It now sits inside City Hall in the atrium entrance.

Addison P. Wyman was born in Cornish, New Hampshire in 1832. He taught music at Stevens High School and composed popular pieces for the piano. In 1868, he composed the Claremont Grand March and performed it in January 1869 with Miss C.A. Bailey at the dedication of the old town hall. This piece was also performed by others at the dedication of the new public building in 1897.

The Claremont American Band was formed in 1888 by Charles H. Perkins and W.F. Jenkins, who recruited area musicians for an all-volunteer community band. In 1897, the band played at the dedication of the new public building. This American Band continues to play Thursday nights every summer on the bandstand in Broad Street Park, under the direction of Ed Evensen.

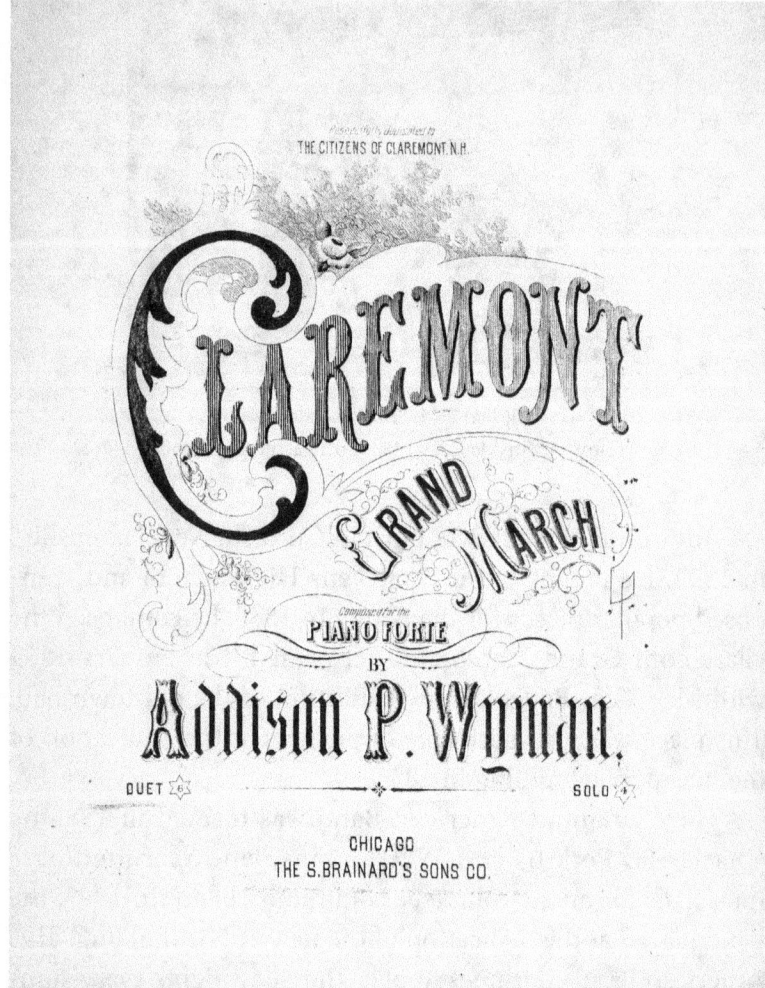

Cover page of the Claremont Grand March sheet music

Claremont American Band, 1897

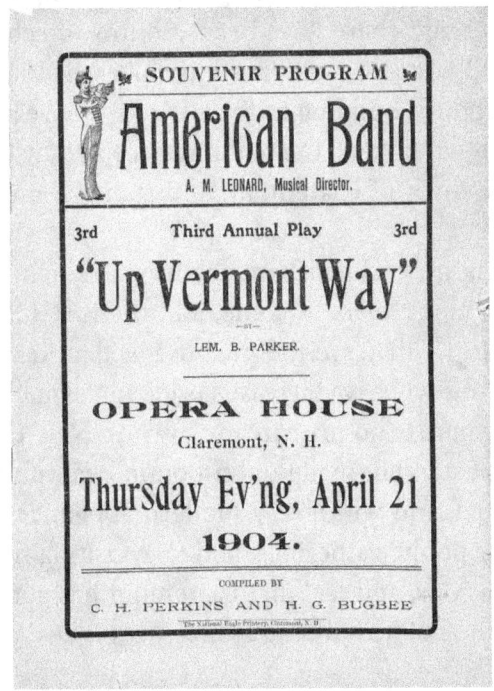

Claremont American Band Program, 1904

Town Hall and Opera House: 1897
These are excerpts from *The National Eagle*, one of Claremont's newspapers at the time, June 26, 1897, reporting on the dedication ceremony.

TOWN HALL DEDICATED.
Interesting Ceremonies in Connection with the New Building
FINE WEATHER AND BIG CROWD FOR CLAREMONT'S GREAT DAY

Claremont has a public building.
A brand-new, up-to-date town hall and opera house. The structure was dedicated to the public with impressive ceremonies, Tuesday. There have been months of scheming and planning and wrangling and hard, thankless work, but that is all passed, and the building is done, the keys have been turned over to the town fathers, the building accepted by them in the name of the town of Claremont, and stands a monument of public spirit.
Providing no accident happens it will remain our public building for many years to come, and the EAGLE trusts and predicts that it will serve the purpose well, and that as time passes everyone will have increased pride to the noble structure, than which there is no finer in any town in New Hampshire.
Solid, substantial, made upon honor, beautifully finished and decorated, and with every modern appliance, we can go there for our public gatherings, and take visiting friends there on gala occasions, and feel that Claremont has got as good as the best in the public building line.

Tuesday was a gala day in Claremont. All fears were early dispelled as to what the weather would be, and no public demonstration was ever lighted and tampered by a fairer June sun.

People were early astir, and as the forenoon advanced, a procession-is-coming atmosphere pervaded the streets.

People from the rural districts and from neighboring towns arrived in teams, on bicycles and on foot. They gathered in groups on the corners, and promenaded through the streets, everybody in their Sunday clothes. From public buildings the stars and stripes were flying, and from numerous windows the national colors fluttered. It produced a regular Fourth of July feeling to walk through the streets.

At 11:15 o'clock the first official demonstrations of the day took place, when the American Band, escorting Chellis Rifles, New Hampshire National Guard, marched through Pleasant Street to the depot.

The Governor was coming. This fact had caused hundreds of curious people to follow the band and soldiers to the depot, where they waited in respectful expectancy.

Promptly at 11:30 the special train from Concord, bearing Governor George A. Ramsdell, members of his staff, regimental officers of the State National Guard, and ladies, rolled into the station. Then, as the executive party alighted from the cars, the band played and the crowd surged forward to get a glimpse of the Chief Executive of New Hampshire. But the police arrangements were good. And the delegation of citizens awaiting the arrival of his Excellency had no trouble nor delay in assigning the visitors to the carriages in waiting.

The Governor was quick to notice the local military drawn up at "Present," and instantly acknowledged the salute. The committee at the depot to receive the Governor were Gen. F.P. Maynard, Hon. H.W. Parker, and M.S. Rossiter, Esq.

Among the turnouts in waiting was the perfectly appointed four-in-hand of State Senator Hastings of Walpole, with the Senator himself on the box. This conveyance was reserved for the Governor and staff, and an imposing load of dignitaries it was, the members of the staff and regimental officers being in full military uniform.

Following the arrival of the distinguished visitors at Hotel Claremont, was a prize drill in Tremont Square by Chellis Rifles. This was interesting, and witnessed by probably 2,000 spectators. The company did well and the competition was sharp, especially when it narrowed to three men, Sargeants Pike and Fitch and Corporal Morrow. The prize was finally won by Corporal Morrow, and presented him by Capt. Edgerly, U.S.A. amidst ringing applause. In presenting the medal, Capt. Edgerly made a neat complimentary speech to the winner.

An exhibition drill without arms, concluded the military part of the day's programme, and it was the unanimous opinion of all that Capt. Timson's men were well drilled, and that a company of state militia was a very appropriate organization to assist in the ceremonies of dedicating the new town hall.

Meantime crowds had been flocking to the south entrance of the hall, in order to secure seats for the afternoon exercises. There was a little delay in opening the doors, and when finally the waiting hundreds were admitted, the seating capacity of the opera house was overreached in a twinkling: Probably 1800 people were seated or standing in and about the auditorium, when President of the day, Hon. H. W. Parker, called the assembly to order, and officially opened the afternoon programme of dedication. It was a scene long to be remembered. Every seat was occupied, making a sea of faces from the orchestra to the entrances. The stage was also closely occupied by invited guests, the building committee, prominent citizens and those taking part in the dedicatory exercises.

The first number on the programme was Weber's "Overture from Oberon," by Eastman's Orchestra of Manchester. This was followed by a prayer by Rev. James B. Goodrich, the great audience standing and afterwards uniting in the Lord's prayer. Then came the opening chorus, and there was a matter of pride at the very start.

After this the entire audience united in the Doxology, and Claremont's new Public Building was officially dedicated. The town hall is achieved; it is a fitting landmark to close the 19th century in the history of Claremont. Let the bickerings, the heart-burnings, the little unpleasantness that have marked the struggles of the building committee and the public, be buried in oblivion, and only peace and good will prevail in the hearts of all.

Following the programme of dedication, a reception was tendered Gov. Ramsdell, in the lower hall, when a large number of citizens shook hands with the Chief Executive.

THE EVENING CEREMONY

The new building lighted up beautifully for the evening programme and presented a [joyful] scene.

At 8 o'clock the opera house was filled, and a few minutes past that hour, the curtain rose for the first time on the drama. There was a murmur of approval as the opening scene was disclosed, and it was difficult to realize that it all belonged to Claremont. "The Burglar" proved an interesting dramatic attraction, and the company of players of a high order. They caused laughter one minute and tears the next, and little Olive Smith as Editha, got right into the hearts of everyone. The lights and stage properties worked without delay or friction, and when the curtain went down on the last scene, it is safe to say a majority of the audience went away satisfied, and anticipating future hours of enjoyment in the opera house.

THE BALL

The day concluded with a ball in the lower hall. It was about eleven o'clock when the strains of a waltz brought the dancers to the floor, and inaugurated the concluding pleasures of the day.

The great hall with its broad polished floor was delightful for, dancing, and the music from Eastman's orchestra, irresistible. Several numbers were applauded by the dancers for a repetition.

There was a large attendance at the ball, and the scene a brilliant one. Many beautiful and elaborate costumes were noted among the ladies present, and a large sprinkling of military uniforms leant life and color to the scene.

The Governor and his suite remained until about midnight, when they took a special train for home. The arrangements for refreshments were nicely conceived. They were announced shortly after the ball opened as being ready in a lower room, and were served throughout the night. They were arranged informally on a long, flower trimmed table, the menu including ices, sandwiches, olives, cakes and lemonade. The catering was under the supervision of H. C. Kimball, and was faultlessly carried out.

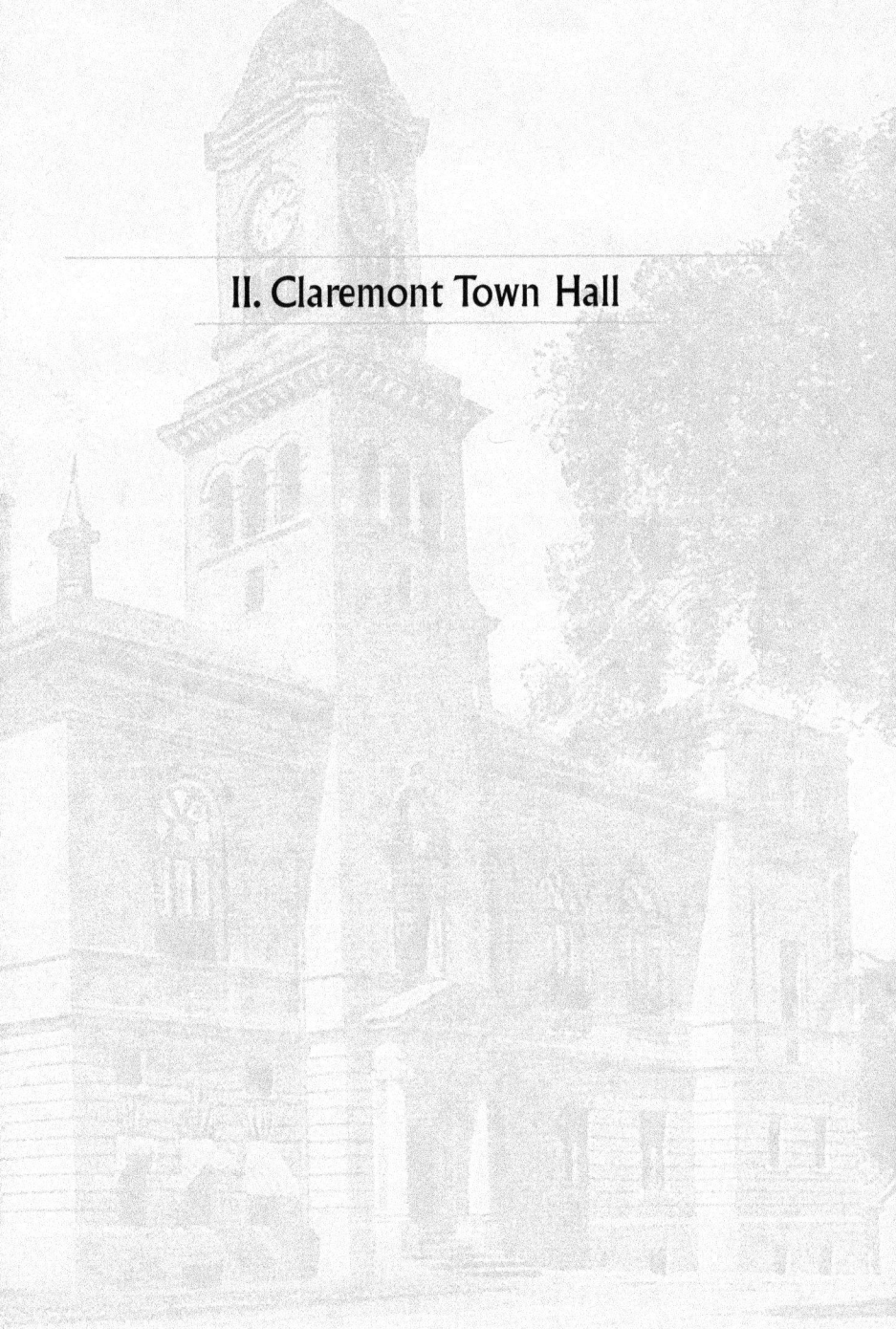

II. Claremont Town Hall

A Sight to Behold

When the building was complete, it was impressive and state-of-the-art. *The National Eagle* described what it looked like when first built:

> From the entrance hall two broad staircases lead to the opera hall, or auditorium, on the second floor, one of the best appointed places for amusement in the State. Comfortable opera chairs afford seating capacity for 661 on the main floor, and for 321 in the gallery, or 982 in all.
>
> The stage is twenty-six feet deep back of the curtain and seventy-two feet wide.
>
> Above all rises the handsome tower, with the illuminated clock. On each floor are waiting and dressing rooms, private offices, electric clocks are also placed in both halls and selectmen's and town clerk's offices.

The floors are of birch except in the two vestibules and the rotunda, where tile has been used with excellent effect. The dressing rooms and coat rooms are finished in North Carolina pine, natural color. The opera hall is finished in bass wood, painted cream color. The assembly hall, the entrance hall, the rotunda, the offices and the main staircases are all in quartered oak.

Most of the windows are of first quality German glass. Some stained glass has been used, and the entrance doors are of plate glass. The building is plastered with adamant. On every floor is hose and adequate provision against fire.

The chandeliers are of bright brass, the general trimmings of bright bronze. All lights on the stage are electric, there being 300 on the stage, and over 400 in the opera hall, entirely controlled by a switchboard in the wings. All over the rest of the building they are a combination of gas and electric, being doubled. (1897)

Keeping in mind that electricity was not commonplace in most homes until at least three decades later, the Opera House must have truly been a sight to behold.

Cynthia McKee remembers seeing the Opera House as a child accompanying her parents to town meetings:

I remember the town meetings were held at the Opera House. I went to the town meetings with my mother and father, and I didn't know what it was all about because I was seven or eight years old, but I spent a lot of time looking at the Opera House interior while I sat there.

They held the meetings upstairs and the moderator and all the officials were on the stage. My most interesting times were when people got angry, and got up, and hollered, and shook their fists and did things like that.

I'd really be quite interested in that. I remember the lighting fixture overhead and also the clock and the marvelous frescoes there, the great faces of tragedy and comedy.

Part of the investment in the Opera House were theatrical stages and sets. Such as this intricate woodland scene.

> When I was older, my mother worked for *The Advocate* and they often had complimentary tickets to the things that went on, and so they would give them to her. We went to a number of plays that were there.
>
> I would not have gotten in there until probably 1920, right along there. But then after my father died, which would've been after 1925, I did go to plays with my mother.

Town Hall

Today's building remains very much the same as it was when completed in 1897—with one major exception. On the ground floor is an entrance lobby which originally led to an assembly hall which seated 700 and was used for town meetings and balls.

In 1960 the south entrance was bricked, and the west entrance altered with glass doors, converting the first-floor ballroom into additional city offices and a council chamber.

When Claremont residents first viewed the building in the late nineteenth century, and for many generations after, their experience was different from that of today:

> The ground floor is entered by a broad entrance into the hall, off which is the assembly hall, 65x63 and 16 ft. high, seating capacity 700. The town offices are in the west front, on the vestibule level. There are large offices for the town selectman and for the town clerk, with vaults in each and private offices. These are remarkably pleasant rooms, commanding, with their wide windows, full views west and south over the business center of the town. (*The National Eagle*, 1897)

The assembly hall was used for dances and other social gatherings, as well as sporting events.

Performers on stage at the Town Hall

Dances and Other Social Gatherings

Cynthia McKee remembers parties from her childhood in the 1920s, where children would dance around a May Pole with colorful ribbon attached to it. The dancers weave in and out to create a pattern down the pole as they dance:

> I went to the May Parties that they had in the Town Hall.
>
> That was always given on the 1st of May and there was a May Ball and then there was a May Pole Dance. That's how I got in there, because all these little girls wound the May Pole.

We had an older woman who always instructed us, and we were not always very easy to instruct, but I can remember being in the May Pole for quite a number of years.

Then I remember many dances there later when I was in high school and afterwards. There was occasionally a square dance, but there were regular dances there.

I would say it had the most wonderful dance floor I've ever seen. It was blonde wood, and highly polished and just beautiful. There were always many folding wooden chairs around the edge. The orchestra would be on the stage.

Before there were big dance halls in Claremont, the Town Hall was the place to kick up your heels. Resident Bertha Emond remembered dancing there:

It wasn't the best floor in town, but it was good.

As I recall, there was a large square with a stage on one end where the band sat. It seems to me that they were posts of some sort, it wasn't a barricade, but it seems to me I recall posts which held up the roof, I suppose.

It was extremely simple. Just folding chairs. There was no attempt to dress it up. It was just where you went to dance.

> It was usually the local band, you know, it was small, probably Frank Bush and the Yacht Club Band. He used to be called the Nighthawks. It was just good music and the crowd used to go. Sometimes it would be so crowded, you could hardly dance. It was good attendance.

The Town Hall served multiple uses over the years, and once other venues in town were built for entertainment and dancing, the Town Hall's uses became increasingly diversified.

Cynthia McKee remembered:

> Some little plays and things, I think, may have been given there too, you know, rather than in the Opera House. It was not a very grand place in the sense that the chairs were hard and folded up.
>
> Then for a long time the Town Hall was used as a polling place, they set up all the booths there. And I think that probably it was the only polling place until we had the three wards, until we became a city. I'm sure that's where my family went to vote.

Sports in the Town Hall

The Town Hall, with its large floor and high ceilings, was also an ideal location for sporting events. Both male and female, professional and amateur competed here.

Bertha Emond: "I've heard people talk of basketball games there, too, and wrestling. They had roller skating there too downstairs in the Town Hall. We used to go roller skating there."

Cynthia McKee: "They played basketball in there and they had boxing matches, which I don't think I got to very much. I barely remember one."

High School Sports for Boys and Girls

Mable Cutting, a 1927 Stevens High School graduate, remembers that her team practiced and competed at the high school itself, with one special exception. She described the practice space at the high school in the mid-1920s versus practicing at the Town Hall:

> What is now the principal's office and the secretary's office, you take those rooms and then room 101, which is the next room where there's a stage: that was our assembly hall. That's also where we played basketball. We had a big net that went over it. It was not the biggest place in the world to play basketball.
>
> There was only one team; no varsity, junior varsity, freshman, or anything. There was just one team: one boys' team, one girls' team. The same coach, Coach Parker, coached both teams, as well as doing all the other coaching. We didn't have separate coaches.
>
> When we got into the tournament, we were allowed to practice down at the city hall. So, we'd get dressed at the high school, run down to city hall in the

wintertime and practice there because there was more room.

When we got to practice for the tournament, we were allowed to play against the boys, practice against the boys. And one of those who practiced against us has told us that we were not the best players, because when it was a jump ball, they said that we always put our fingers over the loops in their shorts, so they couldn't jump as high as the rest.

We played boys' rules, which were much more fun than girls' rules. In the fall of 1926, we were the first girls to have shorts to play in, which was quite controversial.

We'd always worn big bloomers before that. I still have the uniform, but I can't get into it. Then when we went out of town, the girls would get into one car and the teacher would go with us for chaperone. And then the boys would go in another car. That year I think the biggest game we played was Sunapee. We beat the girls in Sunapee 70 to nothing, which was quite something at that time.

Then when we went to Windsor to play in the tournament, we were runners-up. The year before they had been champions, but we were runners-up and our girl Buella Guild was the outstanding player at that time.

> We went up and roomed and stayed in parents' homes. This was in all New England because the players came from Connecticut and Massachusetts. It was not just a Connecticut Valley Tournament.
>
> I can assure you, we had a lot of fun playing basketball.

Paul Mason also remembered playing basketball in the Town Hall, against some prominent players of the day:

> We had a heck of a good basketball team there, back in the '20s. It was just a Sullivan Machinery team. We had a city league, and then we had a league in this whole part of the state. A lot of Dartmouth guys used to come down and play with us. They had to play under assumed names because their status as athletes up there would've been [compromised] if they hadn't.
>
> There were no seven-feet-tall guys. We had these strange knee pads. This is due to the fact that most of the halls we played in around had these registers. They had these registers in the floor and you'd slide across those about twice on your knees and you didn't have any knees.
>
> We played the Original Celtics. There were some guys who came out of Globesville, New York, five guys. And they were the Original Celtics and they toured New England. Every time they came up here, we played them. That was along in the twenties sometime.

But there were people that we shouldn't have been monkeying with because they were not very gentlemanly athletes. It was a lot of fun. I weighed right around 150 then, which is a little light to be playing in that class.

There were rules of a sort. This is when they broke the back of basketball for me. They had what they call a double dribble. You could dribble with two hands all over the floor. And the captain in the team, he weighed about 215, and he was big all over. If he got a little tired, sometimes, all you have to do is just dribble down and flip it to him. And he would get his bottom up in the air and double dribble just around gently around. Nobody could get at him. Nobody could come in. He was surrounded on all sides by muscle and hard tissue, that's one of the things that broke the game up for me.

Then another thing. After every basket, you had a center jump in those days. It wasn't a foot race. It's become a foot race now. The ball was up for grabs after every basket because of the center jump.

We played in the Town Hall. They had some great big backboards, like we have sometimes for hitting tennis, huge boards like that. The night they had the game, they put in all the seats on either side and all around the hall and put up these two backing boards. And then we played in the center of the thing and when it was all through, they carted the baskets away.

SPOTLIGHT

Claremont: A Center of Sports Activity

Sports have a long history in Claremont, but not only at the Town Hall. Earl Bourdon, a lifelong city resident, recalls the days when Claremont was a "major sports center." So much so that as a professional wrestler, his father Eli Bourdon moved from his native Woodstock, Vermont to Claremont to follow the action.

Earl Bourdon recalls:

> My father was a wrestler and later became a sports promoter.
>
> Since his young adulthood, my father was a professional wrestler. At one time he was recognized as one of the middleweight champions of the world in wrestling. He wrestled all over the northern

part of New England and in Connecticut and Massachusetts too.

I saw him wrestle only once. I'm the baby of the family and he had retired as a professional wrestler before I was old enough to remember. I do remember seeing him wrestle only once in about 1926, or seven.

I saw him come out of retirement to wrestle a man named Joe Daley, who had come to this country from England. He was the lightweight champion of the British Empire and a world champion of England. He wrestled my father here in the old Town Hall in the middle twenties, the only time I ever saw him wrestle.

It may seem odd today to think of Claremont as a major sports hub, but with its diversity of venues, it knew how to draw a crowd:

> Claremont was always a tremendous sports town. As long as I can remember, and that goes back to at least when I was 10, Dad ran professional wrestling matches in the place they called the Star Theater. He ran wrestling matches there for years. Then afterwards that became

a combination pool room-bowling alley. Later, he promoted events in both the Town Hall and the Opera House — sometimes outdoors in a tent.

Not only was professional wrestling and boxing important here, but in those days they also had very good semi-pro basketball teams and semi-pro baseball teams. Claremont was just a great center of sports activity.

In the early thirties, maybe as early as 1931, my father ran an elimination tournament to determine who was to be the 147-pound boxing champion of the state. Most of the elimination fights after the preliminaries were held in the Opera House.

The final fight to determine who the state champion was, was between a black fighter that my father managed named Bobby Suber and a French Canadian from Nashua named Wally Theroux. They fought upstairs in the Opera House to jam-packed audiences—standing room only.

On other occasions, I can remember him running boxing matches downstairs in what was then the old Town Hall. I can remember him running wrestling matches in both places when the heavyweights were the important wrestlers. Several wrestlers who came were recognized as heavyweight wrestling champions.

There was some difference between that period when he was running sports than it was earlier when he ran them at the Star Theater. When he was running wrestling matches at the Star Theater, the most famous and active of professional wrestlers were middleweights. Many of them, for one reason or another, claimed championships.

I can remember not having seen any of them but knew later in life that wrestlers like Peter Sturgis were all ranked in the first eight to ten in the world as middleweights. And they all wrestled at the old Star Theater.

Killer Kowalski wrestled in the Town Hall

The peak time for wrestling and for all sports promotion in Claremont, really, in terms of professional wrestling and boxing was that period between 1927 and 1935. There had been promotions after that, but not with anywhere near the intensity or frequency as they were before 1935.

We lived out on a farm and the boxers used to run when they were training and stop at the house. So, I knew all of the boxers as though they were my own personal friends, even though I was a kid. I used to run with them when they ran in their training exercises.

Sometimes in those days, when they signed contracts for important fights out of town, there was a contract stipulation that they had to be in the city in which they were fighting twenty-four hours ahead of time. So, my father used to let me go up a day early with the fighters. I'd stay overnight with them.

Several decades later, Earl's nephew Philip wrote an article in *The Eagle Times*, a tribute to his grandfather's legendary legacy:

> Eli E. Bourdon was born in 1873 in Woodstock, Vermont. His father, Leander Bourdon, was a French-Canadian immigrant from outside Montreal who went on to fight in the Civil War out of the Vermont Regiment.
>
> Like so many in those days, he dropped out of school at a young age. He had developed a powerful build and took work in physically demanding jobs in

factories (he was about 5'7" and weighed 160 lbs.).

He developed his body to such an extent that in the early 1890s he became a professional wrestler in the middleweight division. Those were the old days when professional wrestling was still essentially legitimate (like in boxing a fix was always a possibility). Of course, it helped to have some personality and color in your style, but wrestlers were still overwhelmingly "shooters" and not simply entertainers like they have been for so long ("shooters" as in "straight-shooters").

One story that I loved to hear from dad was how one night there was a quick and unpopular result in the boxing main event. A lot of money was lost on bets and talk rapidly spread that there had been a fix and that perhaps the promoter had profited by it. In the dressing room Grandpa's friends told him that trouble was brewing and that there was a crowd that wanted his hide. They suggested that he should make a break for it out the back door. For Eli E Bourdon, that was not a possible option.

He told his friends, "I have no reason to hide or run away and nothing to fear. It was a square fight and I'm not about to back down."

Of course, it didn't hurt that Grandpa was the most powerful man in the building, but what motivated him was if he had run a show that was legitimate, he had nothing to apologize for. So, despite the anger and "heat" in the crowd, when he walked out of the dressing room, he put his shoulders back and held his head high. In fact, he walked more slowly and deliberately than normal so that he could look the men straight in their eyes. He said in a loud and distinct voice, "Hello boys, thanks for coming out." With the most aggressive looking ones, he extended his powerful hand to give theirs a shake, saying their name and thanking them. He accurately anticipated that they would not resist that. The men, who had been crowded closely together, literally stood aside to let him pass through. So, besides his courage to stand up for himself, he clearly knew how to influence people.

Of course, there were other stories regarding his strength. One was that

Grandpa placed his heels and head on two chairs and was able to support a 200 lb. man carrying a 70 lb. weight on top of him (I was pleased as that story was confirmed in an article focusing on him from the Boston Globe 9/24/1900 which noted quite a few of his feats of strength).

Near the end of my reading about forty articles was one from the Woodstock, Vermont newspaper, Spirit of the Age dated 07/27/1907 (My Dad would have been just one month old at the time, while Uncle Earl was not born until ten years later). I'll allow the article to speak for itself.

> Eli Bourdon of Claremont, New Hampshire, an athletic son of Leander, who is well known here, put his strength to heroic use the other day in stopping a runaway and probably saving several lives. A Claremont dispatch says:
>
>> A circus parade was coming down Tremont to Broad Street, when a pair of heavy horses attached to an ice wagon

frightened by the elephants, ran away and were starting down the easterly side of Broad Street when Bourdon caught their heads and managed to turn them into the Sullivan House stables, where they were stopped.

Bourdon, who is a powerful young athlete, had a narrow escape from death, but refused to accept any praise saying he was thinking of the children lining Broad Street.

On that hot July day in 1907, one of those moments in life came, a challenge that appears where there is no time to think, consider, or ruminate; no time to count the cost or perhaps to even reconsider. It was one of those moments when who the person is inside, his character, his courage, and his spirit is forced to be disclosed by circumstance. In this case, it was revealed right in front of the whole town. I'm proud to say that Eli Edward Bourdon's character was tested and proven on that day, in those moments.

After his wrestling career ended, he promoted both wrestling and boxing matches. Over the years he was able to attract nationally known boxers and wrestlers, including world champion Ed "Strangler" Lewis, a wrestling immortal. He was able to give the local people great entertainment and attract highly rated professionals because of the way he conducted his business. His motto was, "If you don't keep your word and do your best for the boys who fight for you, they won't satisfy the customers who pay their good money for an honest bout." (from the *Claremont Eagle*, 12/5/1944)

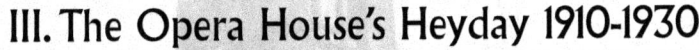

III. The Opera House's Heyday 1910-1930

The Opera House's Heyday 1910-1930

In the early 1900s, the Claremont Opera House was *the* entertainment center for the area. Helping make this a reality was a Claremont druggist named Harry Eaton. Eaton managed the Opera House for thirty-two years. He brought stock companies for plays, road companies for one night stands, musicals, vaudeville, minstrel shows, lecture series, and films. Local musical, theatrical, and political events also took place at the Opera House.

Frank Bush recalled:

> At first local talents, such as The Minstrel Show put on by Claremont's American Band dominated the entertainment portion of the Opera House.
>
> In 1898, Mr. Harry T. Eaton was appointed business manager and soon well-known musicians, singers, and actors began to appear at the Opera House.

Harry T. Eaton, Claremont Opera House Manager
from 1898-1930

A recent review by Ms. Eleanor Colby illustrates the high type of performance presented by the Opera House in its heyday.

In the town's annual report of that year, one finds more than fifty shows took place adding $1,500 to the town's coffers. Among the grand operas, light operas, and operettas were Verdi's *Aida*, Balfe's *Bohemian Girl,* and Mascagni's *Cavalleria Rusticana* by stars of the Boston Opera Company.

The Boston English Opera Company presented *Robin Hood*, Robert Mantel and Genevieve Hamper, exponents of Shakespearean and classic plays, in *The Merchant of Venice*, Victor Herbert's *Babes in Toyland*, and Lee and J.J. Shubert's *Blossom Time*.

Music and sound effects were made live from the back of the screen, to accompany silent movies such as the Lyman Howe Travel and Moving pictures.

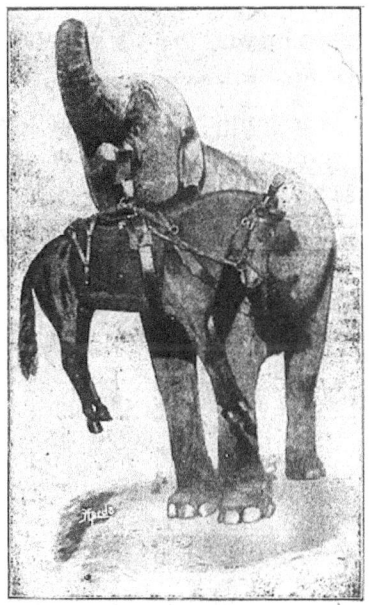

Minnie, the three tonne elephant, a feature of the Aborn Comic Opera Company's spectacle *The Chimes of Normandy* at the Claremont Opera House, Thursday evening, Sept. 18, 1913.

Uncle Tom's Cabin came every year, and matinee prices for children were 20 cents.

Special trains would run from Newport to accommodate patrons desiring to see such an extravaganza as *The Chimes of Normandy*.

Claremont's Opera House was one of the few north of Boston that could handle such a large cast. The show company brought a three-ton elephant with them, and it was remembered by the late Bill Bateman that they tried to hoist him up to the second story by a horse-drawn pulley, but the elephant would have none of it. So, they finally walked the elephant up the front stairs, down the aisles of the Opera House, and up on the stage.

This attests to the fact that the building was of solid construction.

In 1919 the Metropolitan Opera Company presented a recital, and direct from Rome came the world-famous Sistine Choir. A fine pit orchestra was directed by Andrew Leonard.

John Philip Sousa, and his famous band, played a matinee concert on April 10th, 1906.

The chorus line in one of the many home talent shows, local and area actors and musicians presented an operetta directed by M.F. Colby.

When Blackstone, the great magician, came to town, he gained publicity in the afternoon by being chained and nailed in a wooden box that was lowered over the Broad Street Bridge into the Sugar River. He escaped unharmed in time to put on the evening performance.

Boxing and wrestling matches drew large audiences in the lower Town Hall. One wrestler that attracted much attention was Ida Mae Martinez champion lady wrestler of Mexico.

Buster Keating, and his orchestra played for dances in the lower Town Hall.

One of the last worthwhile theatricals to appear in 1926 was Abie's *Irish Rose*. It came here directly from New York after a five-year successful run on Broadway.

Abie's Irish Rose is a popular comedy by Anne Nichols that has become familiar through repeated stage productions, films and radio programs. The basic premise involves an Irish Catholic girl and a young Jewish man who marry despite the objections of their families.

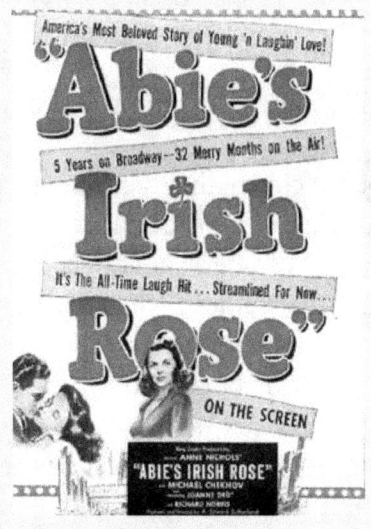

Toward the end of Mr. Eaton's reign as manager and impresario of the Opera House, road shows became scarce. So, he turned to some of the important silent movies of the time: DW Griffith's *Birth of a Nation* featuring Lillian Gish, and Douglas Fairbanks in *The Thief of Bagdad*, as well as Mary Pickford in *Daddy Long Legs*.

Mr. Eaton retired in 1930. Much of the history and information about the Opera House during Harry Eaton's years as manager came from programs and experiences furnished by my father, William Bush. He was Mr. Eaton's assistant manager and treasurer from 1905 to 1930.

Elephants and Donkeys, Oh My!
Though some of the early shows were, in fact, operas, the Opera House has been home to a variety of events—bringing in even, yes, elephants.

Resident Effie White, a Claremont resident from 1901 to 1992, recalls *The Chimes of Normandy*, the famous "elephant show," a comedic opera to which the production company added animals:

> I remember of course the stage seemed to be quite adequate for a large production. *The Chimes of Normandy*, you've heard about that, of course, with the elephant that came? Elephants and ponies, up on the stage. That was a sight, I hope to tell you. Haven't you heard about that?
>
> It was a musical comedy or musical play or something of that sort. It was the beginning of these musicals

that we have all the time now, but it was extremely interesting, exciting, nice voices and all that.

But the donkey, they walked up those stairs, and up onto the stage. I didn't see that, but I saw it going down because they were going to leave after the thing was over.

So, they were getting rid of the elephant; it was really a part of the show. And the trainer asked people to sit quietly in their seats, to make no overtures or noises. Really, it was dramatic in a way, cause the elephant is so ponderous and so particular about putting its feet down. I can't imagine how it could climb up the stairs, but to go down and shift its weight would take some human reasoning, almost, wouldn't it?

Abracadabra

No entertainment venue would be complete without its magicians, and the Opera House has seen its fair share. One of the most notable to perform on the Opera House stage in its early days was Blackstone the Magician, also known as The Great Blackstone.

Charles Chandler, a lifelong Claremont resident, remembers the performance:

> I went to probably four or five shows at the most. I wasn't sold on them. I saw Oh Baby of 1922; it was a musical that came up through here. It was a lively show, well worth watching.

I saw Blackstone the Magician. While I happened to go to the shows 'cause I sold the tickets down there at the store in my senior year.

And then I worked the afternoons going to help put the scenery up. So just to get it up from the Depot, up to the Opera House, up against the wall. And then the regular stagehands took over at night, and they called it striking the flats and they had all these terms.

So, when Blackstone came, I helped set up some of their stuff. I remember he had a ball of fire that he'd have come across the stage, and he'd make it move.

I remember that afternoon, there was a wire running along and that ball ran on that wire. He had me grease it up well, so it wouldn't squeak or anything. Course that takes a thing out of it when you know how they do it.

He had somebody disappear, you know, they'd put something around him and, and they're gone. I knew there was a trap door on the floor there, a little chute that went down to the dressing room down below. I'd gone down through it as a kid. I'd try everything there, all the back stairs and things.

And some of those show girls there, they were kind of rough talking. I didn't hang around too much. I was too young to, I hadn't got to the girls' stage at that time. I was too busy in school, anyway.

Today, TED talks are a popular form of entertainment, but long before they came along, lecture series were popular forms of entertainment. In the heyday of the Opera House, there were many lectures. Effie White also remembers these:

> They used to have lecture courses, you know, and I always had a season ticket. I wouldn't miss it for anything.
>
> Catherine Ridgeway. She was a woman who was a reader, and she was very clever, very funny.
>
> There was an extremely famous, noted man, a Jew who came here to talk. I was most impressed by him of just about anybody I've ever heard. He had come straight from Israel to talk to us in excellent English.
>
> He spoke about Jewish affairs and [Israeli] outlooks and the way they are accepted or not accepted here or there. He was tall, stately, and very impressive.

Lectures were not limited to the Opera House, though. In the late 19th and early 20th century, a social movement centered on adult education set up tents in cities and towns across the country for assemblies called Chautauquas, named after the place in New York where they began. Chautauquas brought speakers, mostly specialists of the day, whose content was considered moral, wholesome, and cultural.

William Jennings Bryan, a three-time Democratic presidential nominee, state representative and Secretary of State under President Woodrow Wilson, was a popular speaker on the circuit, and spoke here in Claremont.

Albert D. Leahy Sr., a 1921 Stevens graduate and local lawyer and judge, remembers the Chautauquas:

> One of the other things they used to have was Chautauquas up here in the high school yard where the new building is. They used to have a Chautauqua tent up there. That would go for several days, a week, or probably four days.

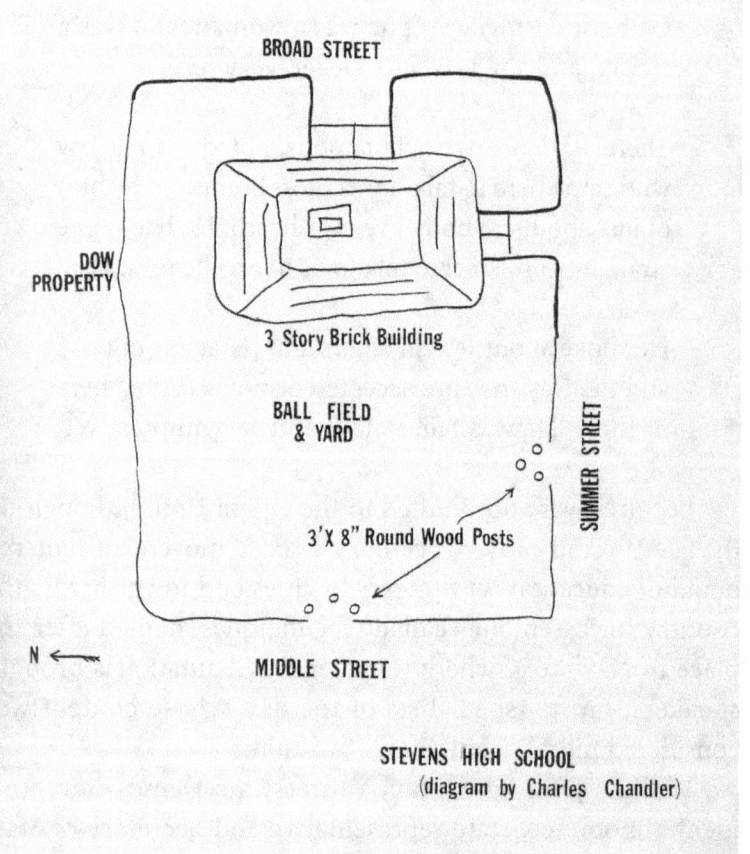

Diagram of Stevens High School by Charles Chandler showing the ball field and yard where Chautauquas took place.

They'd have it be uplifting. It was a concert series, or a singer, or William Jennings Bryan, some speaker.

Mable Cutting also remembers the Chautauquas:

> I went to two or three Chautauquas, and the ones that I went to were musical, but they must have had plays as well. It was a big tent, as I remember. I think that Mrs. Steinfield here in town used to play on the Chautauqua circuit years and years ago. Whether she ever played here or not, I don't know. As I remember, there were musicals and plays. Whether they came for a week, I don't remember.
>
> They were really nice entertainment. It was entertainment that you wouldn't get anywhere else. Anyone that played the Chautauquas, they had to be good.

In the first three decades of the 20th century, tents in fields brought some entertainment to Claremont, including plays. Mable Cutting remembers a play in Monadnock Park:

> Someone came in and put on a play that was down in Monadnock Park. This must have been in 1923 or four. I remember that they had different groups that were supposed to dance the dances of different countries. There was a play that went with it. I was one of the girls that danced in the Irish group, and this is how I happen to remember that.

Yet the Opera House was still the entertainment tour de force in the city. In its heyday, the Opera House was both significant and a part of everyday life. Leahy describes attitudes at that time:

> The Opera House was the same as it is today, but with more things happening there.
>
> The Opera House was the center. We'd have all kinds of good plays there. All these musical comedies, *No, No, Nanette*, and all these road shows would come.
>
> It was the center.

Mable Cutting expressed a similar view:

> It was just accepted that as part of Claremont, I don't remember anymore other than it had always been there.
>
> The Opera House at that time was really the center for better entertainment, I would say. It was all reserved seats.
>
> The Opera House was really the center of the nice entertainment that we had at that time.
>
> It was special. Whatever we attended, it was a big treat.

Effie White's mother ran a boarding house in Claremont called The Fitchburg House. Many performers stayed there:

Back then, the Opera House was the only place to go. I don't know as I talked with anybody about their attitudes about the Opera House; I know I was very pleased with the place.

Here's another thing where The Fitchburg House came in. Road shows came here that would be here a whole week, you know? And if my mother had room for them, they always applied to my mother's house for room. And they were very interesting people, you know? I mean, people that you could talk with nicely, and they had nice things to say and like that. And they seemed to be pleased to be in a place.

There was no such thing as restaurants or anything of that kind. Those days, you know, there wasn't any place you could stop in and have a cup of coffee or donut or anything of that kind. You went for a meal somewhere, to a boarding house. And those, that type of people was awfully interesting 'cause to me they'd been around and seen things, you know, been to different places that I'd heard of, but never expected to see.

The Opera House was a fixture in the city, and in residents' lives for decades. Bertha Emond describes:

> When you ask about attitudes at the time about the Opera House, you're reasoning this from now, when it's a rare thing. It was just part of our lives, and we didn't have an attitude when we went. We

just went to the Opera House, period. It was just there.

> **First Three Productions at the Opera House**
>
> 1. "The Burglar" a play June 22, 1897
> 2. Twenty-seventh Stevens High School Commencement June 25
> 3. Corbett and Fitzsimmons Boxing Match, Acmegraph Veriscope Motion Picture July 10

Ten Cent Shows?

So, the Opera House hosted regional and national acts, serious works and whimsical—in short, a broad range of entertainment. Since its inception, though, one of its important functions has been to host local productions—whether local dance schools, the Rotary Revels or high school plays.

Mable Cutting remembers:

The Opera House really was a lovely place to go, and the entertainment was always good. The high school always put their senior play at the Opera House because they didn't have any other place to do it at that time.

When the high school play was put on at the Opera House, you had to buy your tickets and then exchange them at Glidden's Drug Store for a seat in the Opera House. So, they were all reserved at that time.

Melodie Merrill local dance teacher with her dance troupe on the Opera House stage

> Now, whether those at the other entertainments were reserved or whether you bought them that night as you went in, I couldn't remember all that.

Purchasing tickets at a drugstore may seem a bit odd, but it all makes sense once one understands that the manager of the Opera House also worked in that local pharmacy.

What the modern audience may find even more shocking, however, are the ticket prices. Elizabeth Bell, who resided in Claremont nearly all her life, remembers:

We'd pay 10, 20, and 30 cents, and for 20 cents, we'd get a good seat. We'd go a couple of nights 'cause they'd be there the whole week.

It was nice. We used to enjoy it. They used to have shows that come; I forget the names of it now, but they'd come.

Ten-cent tickets—now that's really something. The system Eaton devised for selling the tickets, by using a model of the interior of the Opera House, was ingenious as well.

Cynthia McKee describes her memories of purchasing opera house tickets as a child:

> You would go in [the drug store] and Harry Eaton would get behind a counter and show you this little mockup of some kind. It seemed to me that it was really a little model of the Opera House. There were all these little tickets stuck up in various places, and you could show him where you wanted to sit and he would pull the tickets out of the model, give it to your father, and he would pay the money.

Charles Chandler was a high school student in the early 1920s and worked at the pharmacy:

> Glidden's Drug Store was one of the best in town, one of the top-quality pharmacies. It was right down near the Hotel Moody, right next to it, right in that block.

It was a drug store. They had a soda fountain, an old-fashioned soda fountain. And they had candy and stuff, cigarettes and things.

They also handled the [Opera House] tickets. Harry Eaton worked there, and he was a manager for the Town Hall for shows and things. So, they sold all the tickets for shows in that drugstore.

He used to book all the shows that came up through here and for the Opera House.

They'd make a stop here in Claremont, in between Boston and Montreal. And so that's how I got in on some of that show business.

He and I got along good. One time I brought my horn. We were in the first band in high school. All we had was secondhand instruments, and I played an E-flat tuba: boom, boom, boom, boom. Cause it's the easiest one to play, you just followed the beat.

And everything was secondhand and used. We had no uniforms, just regular clothes. I happened to bring it down to the store there. And I was downstairs working, and I heard a boom boom, boom boom upstairs.

I went up and Harry's trying to play my horn. He picked it up. We were like a couple of kids, and we were good.

I'd be working out the counter, you know, in the afternoon. I'd go down after school. I'd be working out there, and be working some problems out, or some physics lessons or something. I'd be at the candy counter, and slide back, and reach in to get a chocolate, you know. I looked around one time. He was standing right behind me, and he says "Tastes pretty good. Don't they?"

He caught me in the act.

He was a very nice man. Very nice. Very honest, man. He missed me when I left. I graduated there in June in 1924 and he says, I wish you'd stay, he says, and learn the business.

He was a quick, nervous man. He used to drive a big Peerless, a big car. He was also the owner, he and Daley, of the Magnet Theatre. He had tenement blocks and tenants.

What else did he do? He had all the billboards. He had something to do with all the billboards around here, the advertising you'd see out in the field, the big ones.

He had other men working for him. He was working for Glidden's. He had the theater and the opera house. Harry was a busy man.

SPOTLIGHT

Claremont Public School in the Early 20th Century

MABLE CUTTING:
You were expected to treat all your teachers with respect. You minded your teachers; you accepted whatever they told you. You accepted your assignments. I think school began, at that time, a little after eight o'clock in the morning. We had a short assembly period.

You always opened with a prayer in school at that time, then your classes. I have forgotten whether there was six or seven classes during the day, and you had so many study periods.

Most everybody went home for lunch. There were very few who brought their lunch. There was no hot lunch provided at that time. You did have a recess in the morning so that you had a time out.

This makes me think there were four classes in the morning, that you had two classes and then a recess, and then two more classes. I think school was out at three o'clock or something like that in the afternoon. So, we had an hour, an hour and a quarter, for lunch.

I think that the teachers, of course, there was some you just didn't care for, but that's typical. But I think we had some excellent teachers. And in fact, there was one teacher teaching Latin, Alice Jessie Lindsay Durward who was teaching Latin when I was there, who had taught when my mother was there, a generation before.

A teacher at that time had to be certified, but you only had to go to college or New Hampshire Keene Normal School for two years. At that time, they didn't have the stiff requirements that you have today.

As to what the requirements were, I don't know. But I do know back in the early 1900s that my aunt was a teacher, and she went to teaching right out of high school. She taught up in Croydon for $3 a week, and she drove from Claremont to Croydon on a Sunday. And if she was coming home, she'd come back on a Saturday, but she had the horse and wagon or the horse and sleigh.

Then she went to Keene after that and took her two years so that she was accredited to teach in the schools. She taught in Claremont after that, but there were not too many local teachers at that time. In fact, I think Mr. Dow was probably the only local one that taught at that time in high school.

They didn't make much money, I don't believe, but as for those times, it was good, average pay. If any of them got a thousand dollars a year, that was good pay because in the 1900s expenses weren't as much by any means.

The teachers did take part in public activities, and many of them were involved in anything that was going on for the bettering of the community, but I don't think that I came in contact that much with the teachers outside of school. Whether my parents did I just don't know.

I'd like to speak about going to Bartlett School, which was a little one-room schoolhouse where I started school. That was on Route 11 about three miles and a half outside of Claremont. It was a one-room schoolhouse. In the front of it, we had the stove and a big sheet metal around it, so we wouldn't get burned on the stove.

There was a woodshed there and a little place to hang your coats. We had no running water, no electric lights. So, each morning two of the boys would take a tank and go to the neighbors' at the top of the hill and get the water supply that we used during the day.

I suppose we had hot lunches at that time because in the wintertime we'd bring food to heat up on the stove so we could have hot soup, or if you wanted to bring an egg to fry or some potato, you could do that, look out for yourself to a certain degree.

There were only sixteen students there at this school, and one teacher. It used to be eight grades, but when I was there, it dropped down to six grades.

The wood was always dumped outside of the school and the kids had to throw it in. This was part of growing up. You did your things at the school: you swept the floors and you dusted. We didn't think it was a hard life, but probably now looking back, they'd think that it was really too bad.

It was an ideal teacher-student setting. It was one teacher with sixteen kids. And, in this way, I was one of the fortunate ones in that we could recite with other classes. I did second and third grade together so that I didn't have to go to school for six years. I only went five.

At that time for a music teacher, we had a Mr. Daniel D. Ladd, and he would come out perhaps once a month or once in two months. I can remember him particularly because he came out on a bicycle, and he had a little motor on it, to help him go up and down the hills. And he had his violin and he brought that out with him. It was a big treat when he brought his violin to play.

We also had a writing teacher that came occasionally, but most of the responsibilities were for the teacher who taught there.

You went to school there until you completed the sixth grade. Then when you went into seventh grade, and I believe it was the same for all of the schools in the surrounding area, we went into North

Street. Those who lived on the north side of the river went to North Street. Those on the other side of the river went to Way School, and they had seventh and eighth grades there.

We had to walk a mile from our house, winter and summer down to the hill to the little Bartlett's School. Then Mrs. Jaques was paid by the city to furnish transportation. So, she would meet us there with a horse and wagon in the summertime, and a horse and sleigh in the wintertime. That was three miles into the village and went to North Street School, and then she'd pick us up and take us home.

I think there were three of us at that time that were brought in. I assume that transportation was furnished for others in the outlying areas, but I just don't know.

Then when you had finished eighth grade, it was a responsibility of the parents to get their students to school, if they were going to high school. If a person had completed the eighth grade, regardless of their age, they were not required to continue school any further. When they were sixteen or eighth grade, they could drop out without any question.

Now they have to continue school until they're sixteen.

My brother used to ride a bicycle back and forth to school, but I only came from the farm to the high school for probably four or five weeks. I used to ride with a Mr. Underwood who worked in the foundry, and he lived at the little place above us. He had to be at work at seven o'clock in the morning, and he worked until six o'clock at night. So, I would get up and ride to work with him, to be here in the village at seven, and then wait until six o'clock at night to ride home with him.

With my extra time, I would either sit in his car and wait, or I'd work at school and I'd get my studying done, which I had to do.

Then we moved into the village and that was the end of when I had to go into the high school. So, this was a change.

If anybody asked me what I remember most was home economics. We had a Mrs. McQuaid, who was a teacher and she taught home economics. All I remember of getting out of that class was I learned how to can tomatoes and make fudge, which I don't think is an essential part of education.

There was fifty-three in our class at the high school. When you went to high school, you had to take certain courses. There were no electives as there are now. You had to take the academic course, the business course, commercial course, domestic arts course, English scientific course, or mechanic arts course. That was programmed for you right straight through. You took those courses and no deviation from them at all.

There were only fourteen teachers in the whole high school and the headmaster, and the sub-headmaster taught as well as being the so-called principal and assistant principal.

The high school at that time was only the front end of the high school. The back part had not been added on. That addition came later, and that was a playground out in back. And the Chautauquas used to have their events there.

I can remember too that those of us who didn't take our dinners, and occasionally you were allowed to bring your dinner, that on the outside of the building, there are little ledges between the bricks. When the boys were real courageous, they would go up those bricks and go in the window, instead of going in and up the stairs as they were supposed to.

If they got caught, they were severely reprimanded for it. We had our get togethers there at the high school. Where we played basketball is what is now called Room 101, which is the large room on the right, as you go in the front door on Broad Street.

We only had hockey and basketball for the girls, and then there was football, baseball, and basketball for the boys. The boys played football down at Monadnock Park. Prior to that, before Monadnock Park was given to the city, they played football at Pine Grove Park out Maple Avenue. If they played Windsor, Windsor would come down by train and then ride the trolley cars into the ballpark. If we played Windsor, they'd ride the trolley to Claremont Junction, take the train to Windsor. When they went to Newport, they'd take the train to Newport.

Sports were a pretty big part of high school. At that time, the boys that played in football or any of the sports for that matter, they were really looked up to and respected a great deal. They were supposed to set good examples for the rest of the students. And of course, Buella Guild, who was our outstanding basketball player was highly respected by everybody. There was a prestige to being chosen to play on the team.

Those who were selected for the teams, they had to try out for it, and they could be eliminated very easily. It was only the better ones that they kept on the teams. I think that sports were a very important part of high school. They did have a band and orchestra at that time, but it was very small.

THE FIRST RADIOS IN CLAREMONT

In the early 1920s home radios became commercially available, and small radio stations were popping up in major cities across the nation. Radio was, however, in its infancy, and a home radio was rare. Mable Cutting recounts her recollection of one of Claremont's first:

> *I remember one thing in high school. We had a Mr. Dow who we always called Pop Dow. He taught us history and also some civics.*
>
> *He was one of the first people in town to have a radio. And if there was anything*

special going to be broadcast on the radio, we'd draw lots in our class as to who would be invited to his home to listen on the radio that night. Now everyone has radio.

The kinds of things that would be important enough to go to his house would be: if there was going to be something special on music, or if there was going to be some speaker who was outstanding, this is when you would get invited.

It only happened probably two or three times during the year, but it was a big event when anybody was invited over there.

How High School Graduation Changed the Opera House

From Stevens' twenty-seventh graduation in 1897 until 1930, the annual graduation and baccalaureate ceremony were held at the Opera House. At that time, the high school building had no room large enough to host such an event, and the Opera House, with its fine acoustics and generous seating, made an ideal venue.

Effie White remembers:

> It was a very enjoyable occasion and, of course, we weren't the only class they had [graduate there] because there was no other place except there.
>
> The acoustics made it perfect. It used to have very fine acoustics, I think. I didn't have any part to read. I wasn't a brilliant scholar, any Cardinal valedictorian, salutatorian or anything like that.

The girl who read the class history was a Charlestown girl. A lot of Charlestown youngsters came up here. There was no Charlestown high school then. And she had a throat disorder of some kind, so I was chosen to read the history.

I had done reading here and there. I can't pinpoint any particular thing, but I seem to have a voice that carried somehow or other, or good enunciation, or something of that sort.

I was chosen to read this history and I was tickled to death. I loved it. I rehearsed it, practiced it at the Opera House and everything, but goodness, that girl, she recovered in time to read her own history. So, I never got the chance.

The graduation was a very important event, looked forward to. The stage was comfortable to be on. It didn't seem crowded or anything like that. It was an easy affair.

A baccalaureate ceremony is one which celebrates graduating seniors. Traditionally, it was a religious, usually Christian, ceremony held the Sunday before graduation. Many modern baccalaureate ceremonies do not necessarily have religious significance or undertones.

A Stevens High School graduating class on the Opera House stage.

Albert D. Leahy Sr. remembered baccalaureate in the Opera House:

> We used to have a high school baccalaureate. We used to march from the high school down to the Opera House. We had baccalaureate down there because that's the only building that was big enough.

What was it like to attend these ceremonies in the Opera House, with its opulence and fine acoustics? Mable Cutting recounted:

> Our high school class was the first class to graduate with caps and gowns. They were heavy, black ones. Before that, they'd been just regular. Girls usually

wore white and boys wore a suit, but we were the first with caps and gowns.

Then a few years later they changed to a gray, and then eventually they came to these lightweight red ones that they have at the present time. Graduation was held at the City Hall, in the Opera House. We had baccalaureate and graduation at the Opera House.

We would all line up at the high school and march down. It was compulsory to attend baccalaureate. You were lined up according to height, you didn't have a chance to select who you wanted to march with or anything. You were just lined up. The tallest ones were in front and, and then it went right down the line.

It was still male and female marching together in 1927, but the tallest boy and the tallest girl were the ones who always came first.

At baccalaureate, at that time, the newspaper published the entire speech of the minister, Reverend Chase, who spoke there at that time. It's a great deal different from what you get in the papers today. But of course, they cover so much more than papers did at that time. So, you can't fault them for that.

I don't really remember anything outstanding that happened at our graduation, but our classes got together every year since for a get-together of some type.

You'd march in and you would march up onto the stage. You would be seated the way you marched in, all the way across. Then the graduation would be with the programs. At that time, they had the orchestra, the chorus, the salutatorian's address, the valedictorian's address; they had a concert by some violinist, a trombone solo, a piano solo, and two or three recitations. One was "Why Women are in Business," and another one was "Electricity Yesterday, Today and Tomorrow." The fellow who gave that speech went on to be quite a noted scientist and developed electricity quite a bit further.

Then Mr. George Merrill, who was the chairman of the high school committee, gave the address and they presented the diplomas. At that time, the high school committee was a separate committee from the school board.

The original Stevens High School is the very front of the building, then the addition was put on at the back, and the first class to graduate from that was 1930, in the new auditorium.

Once Stevens High School built its auditorium, graduation and baccalaureate changed slightly. Cynthia McKee, who graduated from Stevens in 1932—two years after the auditorium's completion—remembered:

> When I first went to Stevens, they had not built on. They were getting ready to build the addition where the auditorium gymnasium is and all of

those classrooms on Summer Street. When I first went there, all of that area where that building is now was a school yard. And it seems to me it had a wrought iron fence around it, as many of the places did in those days.

Of course, we didn't have a gym or anything then, but there was this enormous assembly hall, I guess. There weren't thick seats in or anything. They took all the seats up, from around the edge and there was a little stage there. You can still see the stage that was in it if you go in the music room on the first floor of high school, but the rest of it has been made into offices.

Before I left school, perhaps when I was a sophomore or a junior, the addition was completed.

When we graduated, I don't know that we were the first class, but we were one of the first classes to have our graduation in the gymnasium auditorium.

We had caps and gowns by the time I graduated, I think they were, I'm not sure that they had them when I went into school. I think it was during my four years that that was begun.

A new auditorium—seems a laudable achievement, and surely it was for many reasons. Its construction, however, marked an important milestone in the life of the Opera House. For one, Stevens High School could now host its own events which drew large crowds: graduation, baccalaureate, and school plays, for example. Further, many groups or organizations wanted to use the new venue in town—even though the Opera House, in many ways, remained the superior entertainment venue in the city.

Bertha Emond explained:

> When the Stevens Auditorium was built, that took away some from the Town Hall. That would've been in the thirties.

Other social forces were bearing down on the community as well. The stock market crash of 1929 threw the world into the Great Depression—a time when money, jobs, and food were scarce.

In the city of Claremont, "problems began in the 1920s when the mills folded. By 1920, Claremont had almost half the county population," Professor Jere Daniell, chairman of the Dartmouth College History Department, who served as academic humanist required for obtaining funding for the 1980 Oral Histories Project, explained.

The Opera House was about to face its first major challenge. Daniell also explained:

> While today we idolize the rural village with its white houses and red barns, for them it was the mill town, the Claremonts, the St. Johnsburys, the Berlins. There was a mill town utopia, and Claremont was the center of civilization.
>
> The remnants of the utopian view still can be seen in the elegant opera houses and the Victorian homes dripping with gingerbread.

> But the Depression killed the mills and killed the fortunes of the people who were trying to bring culture in, bringing about the eventual lessening of the mill towns' stature. (Croft 9)

The Great Depression would bring about many changes in the way entertainment was consumed in Claremont, as it did throughout the country and world. Technological advances in film and sound recording would usher in a new era of entertainment as well.

IV: Movies and Theaters in Claremont: A City on the Cutting Edge

Early Days of Movies in Claremont

The opening of the Opera House in 1897 was concurrent with the advent of moving pictures, or what we generally refer to today as movies. Claremont was at the cutting edge of productions at that time.

Today, to film a boxing match seems normal, but in 1897 filming and showing a fight was highly unusual. Therefore, the Claremont Opera House was at the cutting edge of the arts and entertainment scene when it showed *The Corbett Fitzsimmons Sparring Contest*. This was the first motion picture ever shown in Claremont.

The reels were eight minutes long, narrated by a tuxedoed man, and were the third event at the Claremont Opera House, shown right here in our fair city before even larger cities such as San Francisco. (Hawley)

As technology advanced in the film industry, Lyman H. Howe, an early filmmaker began touring his "Travel Pictures." Rather than have a live narrator, these films were narrated by a wax disk played on a phonograph, and sometimes accompanied by live side effects.

The Travel Pictures highlighted such faraway places as India, Europe, and Niagara Falls. (Atticpaper)

Frank Bush recalls seeing these pictures at the Opera House:

> They were good. They would have sound effects from the back of the stage. They would have wind machines, and the manager usually went around. There would be three men: a pianist, the manager, and the operator. It was a portable booth; they put up a canvas. And then the man had to turn the crank. It wasn't electrically operated. He had to turn the crank all the way through, but the manager in back, he'd get a couple of boys. When I was a young kid I used to go. You'd have, for example, waterfalls: you'd have a big cylinder, sandpaper or something, and you'd be turning it around.
>
> The manager did a good job, bringing in the sound effects to go along with it.
>
> That's about all they showed for movies at the Opera House; it was never really set up for movies. The Opera House was built for live entertainment.
>
> The travel shows had all their own equipment, their own screen and everything you see, I don't think they ever had a screen.
>
> The films certainly were entertaining—especially to audiences who had likely never seen moving pictures before, however, the sound still had some catching up to do, in terms of quality.

Silent Films and Claremont's First Theaters

The next stage of film technology is what we now call silent films. The films were not actually silent, as they were accompanied by music and sometimes sound effects, however, they did not feature any talking.

Mable Cutting remembered:

> The first movie I ever went to was at the Star Theater. We went to see *Alice in Wonderland*. We lived on the farm and a lady in town gave us tickets to go to see *Alice in Wonderland*. So, we drove down and that was the first movie I ever saw.
>
> It was silent, because the talkies didn't come until long, long after that. Back in 1927, they were all silent movies.
>
> I can remember, my husband and I, we'd go to one, and then rush madly over to the other one, go to both of them on the same night. I can also remember that they ran serials, and my father took me to the old Tremont. We went to every one of the serials for *The Last of the Mohicans*. Of course, that was a small theater. And at that time, they had the piano player at both places.
>
> There was a Miss Jones that played the piano at the Magnet. And then there was a Mrs. Sanders that played the one at the Tremont. Then the Latchis was built afterwards. I didn't go to the opening, but I did go to the second night over there. That was

a gorgeous affair when it was first opened. It really was quite the beautiful place.

It was very ornate. The paintings on the walls down where the columns were, were very lovely. The ceiling was blue, and the stars were above that and they all sparkled. The seats were very comfortable. They had excellent movies. It really was a place that you enjoy going to.

Many local musicians were employed to accompany the films. Miss Ruth Jones, and her school were well known throughout town.

Claremont Resident Mildred LaPanne remembered:

Miss Jones played the piano. And the violin teacher played the violin. And she taught right there too, Miss Jones.

She also played for silent films. And then they would play faster when the train would go by. Oh, it was awful. I don't know how they ever pieced it together. I had a chance to play and win some money, but my mother wouldn't let me. I was only fifteen.

They would ad-lib the sounds. Miss Jones knew a lot by heart, but she always had a lot of music piled up, ready for the show. And, of course, she had an afternoon show and two in the evening. So, she played the three. And I played it for a week once. I took her place.

Frank Bush played for the orchestra for silent films. He described his experience watching films from the orchestra pit:

> At the time the Latchis opened, it was a beautiful place. They spent a lot of money on it. It was a year or so before the Depression started.
>
> Some of the musicians that came to play there in the pit were in a depressed type of area, but that wasn't due to the Depression. That was due to the talkies coming in, see, before the talkies came in, you had to have live music in the orchestra pits.
>
> In fact, as I had played at the Magnet quite a bit for a couple of years on the feature when they had the feature pictures. Several of us boys that played in the dance band cause the dance bands were mostly on Fridays and Saturdays. They usually would operate the better pictures, the feature pictures, in the early part of the week.
>
> 'Cause they'd get the crowd Friday and Saturday, anyway.
>
> When The Latchis opened, they had a real fine orchestra, but some of the musicians in it had come up here from the cities like Springfield, Massachusetts. They used to drop in the music store, and they had always been thrown out of work down there because of the talkies, and they were going back up to places that didn't have talkies yet, like Claremont, because they came in gradually.

I can remember playing at the Magnet and the news reel would come out with talking. They put on a big record, but the actual movie itself was still silent.

I remember one very good show at the time was *All Quiet on the Western Front*. And I was kind of peeved because during the exciting time you'd have to be playing like mad reading the music and when it was quiet for the love scenes, well then you could watch, because all it was was piano and violin, so I missed all the action.

Here in Claremont, several movie theaters opened to accommodate the growing film industry and its audiences. At one time, there were several theaters available for entertainment, with new theaters popping up around town. Frank Bush explained:

The Dreamland was before the Tremont. The Dreamland was on Tremont Street down where Rowe's Furniture was, and a man named Daley operated that. They had a piano player, and they'd have a singer. They used to run westerns and that type of thing; it was just a small place.

The Star was on Sullivan Street, and it had been an old livery stable. Somebody turned it into a theater, and it wasn't very comfortable. They had these folding wooden chairs in there and they didn't do too well. I think they didn't last very long.

The meantime, the Tremont Theater, there was a smaller place. It didn't take as many people, but it always looked like there was, you know, a full house and they seemed to be quite popular. They were across the street, but upstairs from The Dreamland.

The Original Nickelodeon
Many of us have heard the term nickelodeon. Though for many it refers to a television network of today, its original meaning was for a nickel show—the cost to see a movie back in the early days of silent films.

Charles Chandler remembered:

> You could go to some movies for a nickel those days, all silent pictures. And instead of hearing any words, or anything, they'd be printed. Then they always had a piano player that could play that funny music there at the Nickelodeon.
>
> Then there was the Tremont Theater, and that was a big drawing card for years. So, we had these two theaters. The Dreamland went out of business and the same owners went up and built the Magnet Theatre. Then there used to be a Star Theater in back of the alley uptown in back of Hill's Optician.

Many young people and students can relate to the problem of not having enough money to go to a show. What did kids do in the early days of cinema?

Albert D. Leahy Sr. explained his crowd's solution:

> We used to go to the movies. They used to run the movies for one week, same film. So, we used to peddle bills, all the kids would, and they'd give us a pass to movies.
>
> Course we'd see the same picture, but we were thrilled. We'd get that same picture, but we could go any time we wanted to. So, we'd walk all over town, giving these handbills out for that pass.
>
> The next week you'd hand bills over again and they'd give you another pass. I might have been seventeen or eighteen years old. I don't remember, but I remember going.

Interestingly, many of the theaters which opened had stages to feature vaudeville entertainment—what we might today call a variety show, in which entertainers would sing, dance, perform sketches, juggle, or many other forms of entertainment.

Bertha Emond described her experience with vaudeville in the movie theaters:

> They used to have vaudeville every Sunday night. My husband and I, this was before we were married, used to go faithfully to both the Magnet and the Latchis Theatres, same night. We'd go to the Magnet first, usually, for a movie, and then catch the Latchis vaudeville and movie. Sometimes we'd see the vaudeville twice, right down in the front row.

Charles Emond, Claremont Opera House Stage Manager in the 1950s and Bertha Emond's husband

They used to have five acts on a regular basis. You have a comedian and an animal act, a magic act, dancing, singing, almost always singles or doubles. There were very rarely many more than that in a single act. If you got four or five people, that was a big deal for one act, but they were fun.

Leahy remembered:

The Latchis opened about 1927 or eight. It was movies, but then they got to having vaudeville on Sunday nights. They'd have vaudeville just one night, either Sunday or Saturday night. They wouldn't have it every night.

Mable Cutting added:

I don't know whether they had vaudeville every week or not, but they did have vaudeville then. They also had vaudeville over at the Magnet Theatre as well. When they had the community concerts here, they held those at the Latchis Theatre. And 'cause I remember going there and they had Ferrante & Teicher who are now quite nationally known, and they played the piano there.

With all these theaters competing for audiences, some were destined to fail. Mable Cutting described:

The Star Theater went out; that didn't stay too long in business. It went out during my childhood and then the other two were the ones who came into existence. Of course, the Magnet is burned. Tremont Theater is gone entirely and the Latchis, I guess they use the ground floor.

All of a sudden, talkies came in and that was the end, but that would probably be the latter part of the thirties.

From Silent Films to Talkies
The first talking films were difficult to hear, as the sound was recorded on a wax disk, and voices could be warbled or muffled.
Claremont resident Arthur Garneau explained the experience of viewing such a film:

> Now, the first talking picture appeared here in the Opera House. They called it the Vitaphone. You could hear a sound, but you couldn't make it out. You couldn't tell what they were saying. But I saw that here in this Opera House.

However as silent films gave way to better talkies, the Claremont Opera House experienced its second big shift. With quality entertainment offered to audiences through film, there was less demand for live entertainment.
Frank Bush described:

> When the theaters really began to take over, the Opera House began to go down then, to more or less local talent or local shows that would be put on, but traveling shows stopped. They didn't go anywhere after that. I would say the thirties and the Depression put an end to traveling road shows.
>
> When the movies got good and popular around 19— I'd say 33 or 34—I think that's when the Magnet got big.

I'm not sure on my dates there, but Harry Eaton could see the handwriting out of the Opera House. Talkies coming in, or movies, were beginning to make a change in the audiences at the Opera House. So, he could see that there was a need for a good movie theater, cause all the others were either too small or they didn't get the first rate pictures.

So, he wanted to have a good movie theater—a good big one, of good size, with acoustics on stage, such that you could put on vaudeville if you wanted to. The other theaters couldn't, you see. So, he went to Herbert Daley who had The Dreamland and said, "I don't have time to run it. I'll get the money. I'll see that we can get the loan we need to get started. I know how theaters work. I feel we can do a lot."

He talked him into closing the Dreamland and going in with him, which he did.

They opened the Magnet, and it was quite a theater.

They built the Magnet Theatre. I understand that that block was owned by Colby, the attorney. I guess probably he arranged to get most of the money to start the thing going. I think they did a tremendous business. I think they opened in 1914.

It was *the* theater.

It was very short, but they had a balcony.

The Magnet lasted a while, but not too much longer after that because, after the Depression Eaton wanted out, and Daley had retired. So, they sold the place to the people who owned the Tremont.

Bertha Emond described what the Magnet was like:

> It had three separate sections. There was a second, a middle like this and the two sides sections downstairs, and upstairs.
>
> It wasn't as grand as the Latchis, it wasn't as large, and it didn't attempt any Greek revival sort of thing. It was more Egyptian, the decor was when they refurbished it, they must have aimed at the Egyptian with more or less success.
>
> The balcony was fairly deep again, divided into three as the downstairs was.
>
> My earliest memories of the Magnet go back to very early. I was four or five and I lived with an aunt because my mother was working. And she loved the movies. She'd take me almost every day. I grew up in the movie theater, and we used to go down in the afternoons. They had a matinee every day.
>
> Once in a while, during a period, they used to have amateur shows. And I sang in one of those once. Yeah. We had a trio, and we came in second because they had to have a roller skater that night.

> That was an unusual event, a roller skater on stage. So, he came in first. We were quite perturbed. I was in my teens, which would've been fifteen, in the thirties.
>
> They had that kind of vaudeville, and they used to have special shows. I can remember an Irish tenor coming almost every year, a blind, Irish tenor who used to sing. And I think he got only what he could collect from the audience. Or he used to take up a collection.

One entertainment that remained consistently attended throughout the Great Depression were movies. The tradition of the nickelodeon continued.

Bertha Emond described:

> It was so little, it was 5 cents, 10 cents.
>
> I can remember going, especially in the afternoon, sometimes after school. St. Mary's High School always got out at two, because so many of the people worked. So many of the students had part-time jobs that they always got out earlier at St. Mary's than they did in the public schools. And we used to quite often go to the afternoon show and I can remember going into Houghton's and begging an extra nickel from my mother to compensate for what Charlie [my eventual husband] didn't have to make up a double, you know, 15 cents.

It was very cheap, for the amount of entertainment you got. It was the best thing you could do to spend your money.

Cynthia McKee added:

When I got out of high school, this was deep in the Depression. And I couldn't get a job the first year, anywhere. Until I finally got a job ushering in the Latchis Theatre and the pay, it was $2 a week. It was a grand theater, and it was a lot of fun.

There was another usher, a man, and the theater manager was a man named Joe Belluscio. I believe that he was Greek or Italian. He was a great cheerful, happy-go-lucky sort of fellow.

The usher's job was to go up and ask the patrons where they would like to sit and usher them to their seats. We were equipped with a flashlight, you understand? And when anyone came in, we rushed up to them and we were to ask them where they wanted to sit.

I was not expected to deal with any kind of trouble, I'm happy to say, but I did get to see the movies. And it was a lovely theater. It had a ceiling with the stars. It has stars and clouds overhead. And they had the boxes. It did have lovely velvet curtains. We had vaudeville in those days. And I remember that there was a company, a Shakespearean company, I think it was Maude Adams. They were a traveling company, and they came here once. They did a Shakespeare play, and they needed extras.

So, I got to be an extra. I stood up on a balcony someplace with a lot of other people. It was just lots of fun. I met the actors.

Movies were great, then. You would go early to be sure you got a good seat. And as I said, they had vaudeville on weekends usually. And there might be five acts of vaudeville before a good movie.

Bertha Emond also remembers the Tremont Theater:

During the Depression, my father sold popcorn at the Tremont Theater. I used to get in free. I can remember Saturday afternoon cowboy movies, which I used to love incidentally. But that was one of his Depression jobs.

I don't know when the Tremont folded. I think he worked in the Star for a bit too. It was a long narrow thing with a very brief balcony up at the top. It was just perfectly straight. It looked like a long hall.

Albert D. Leahy remembered:

During the second world war, Dorothy Lamour (who frequently performed with Bob Hope and Bing Crosby, most notably in their *Road* movies) and Cesar Romero came here to sell bonds, so we had to go see them.

They came to the Latchis. Course the place was crowded.

Big Stars in Claremont

Imagine your favorite A-list actors stopping in Claremont to sign autographs. It seems difficult to imagine today, but in the days of the grand theaters here in town, big stars came to visit.

Cesar Romero on a USO tour at the Latchis Theatre on June 9, 1945. He is standing with Walter Hentschel, manager of the Latchis.

Movie Theaters' Impact on the Opera House

As many audiences increasingly spent their time in movie theaters, interest in live entertainment dwindled. The Claremont Opera House still offered varied live entertainment, and its stage also saw an increase in local acts.

As the Claremont Opera House once again dealt with a shift in audiences, local theater groups, and other organizations were featured on its stage.

Cynthia McKee remembered:

> I remember the backstage too because after I was out of high school, professional directors would come here and put on a play with local talent. It would just be one man would come here and he would have a musical or whatever, and he would draft all these people to be in it and throw it together much the same as the Cardiac Capers.
>
> Lots of young people were in it and we really had a ball. There was a chorus line and there were all

these skits, and sometimes it would be a little plot to the thing. So, I was at the Opera House a lot backstage, and the dressing rooms downstairs were not too clean. All the place was really dirty.

But, well, not so bad that you couldn't use it. And I remember that you could go from the lower level where the dressing rooms are. You could go down into the Town Hall from there too.

Maybe we used the dressing rooms if we were in something that was on the stage down there, I just don't remember. But it was very exciting, I thought. We would have an orchestra down in the pit the same as we did for the marvelous grand opening that we had. It was a local orchestra, of course.

And I can remember how encouraging it was to me. Frank Stone, who was really a fine musician, would put together an orchestra for these things. And I especially remember him because I can remember being on the stage and being nervous and hoping I was going to do all right. And looking down at his wonderful face that seemed to say "You're just marvelous; you're doing fine." And that was just very reassuring. I will never forget him.

The Claremont Dramatic Club was active for a great many years, sort of like the Ashley Players. We probably weren't as good, but we thought we were. Right out of high school, I was invited to join that. They needed a very young woman and a very young man. So, I guess by virtue of being in the senior play or something, I got invited.

I had a wonderful time. They were older people and did all kinds of things. They had been doing all of their plays at the Opera House, and I can't really remember whether I was in one that was at the Opera House or not. It seems to me there was a great variety of things going on. It wasn't open every week or every day, but it was pretty regular, something happening at the Opera House that we went to.

It wasn't on its way downhill when I remember it, perhaps it was to a certain extent, but there was a lot going on there.

I also remember the Rotary Revels.

Bertha Emond described The Rotary Revels:

They were variety acts usually, people getting up and doing what they could do. Barbershop quartets. We had a few of them. Skits, usually home manufactured. As far as I knew they wrote their own, they may have gotten them out of French's plays or something, but I don't know. They were always great fun of course, because there were people you knew, and they almost always referred to other people you knew somewhere during the evening.

V. The Changing Scene of Music and Dance

Pine Grove Park

Though the ballroom at the Opera House remained a popular venue throughout the first half of the twentieth century, additional venues popped up around town. The first of those was Pine Grove Park.

Charles Chandler also recalled the venue:

> My wife and I used to go to Pine Grove Park. That was out on Maple Avenue where all those houses are built on that right hand side; that was a great big park full of pine trees. It was very pretty, of course. The trolley ran out there. The trolley used to run from Claremont Junction up around, through, and down Pleasant Street.
>
> So, Pine Grove Park was just a matter of getting on the trolley.
>
> They had a baseball field. They had a moving picture house out there, and they had a big dance hall. It was a *big* dance hall. It was one of the first to have a crystal ball.

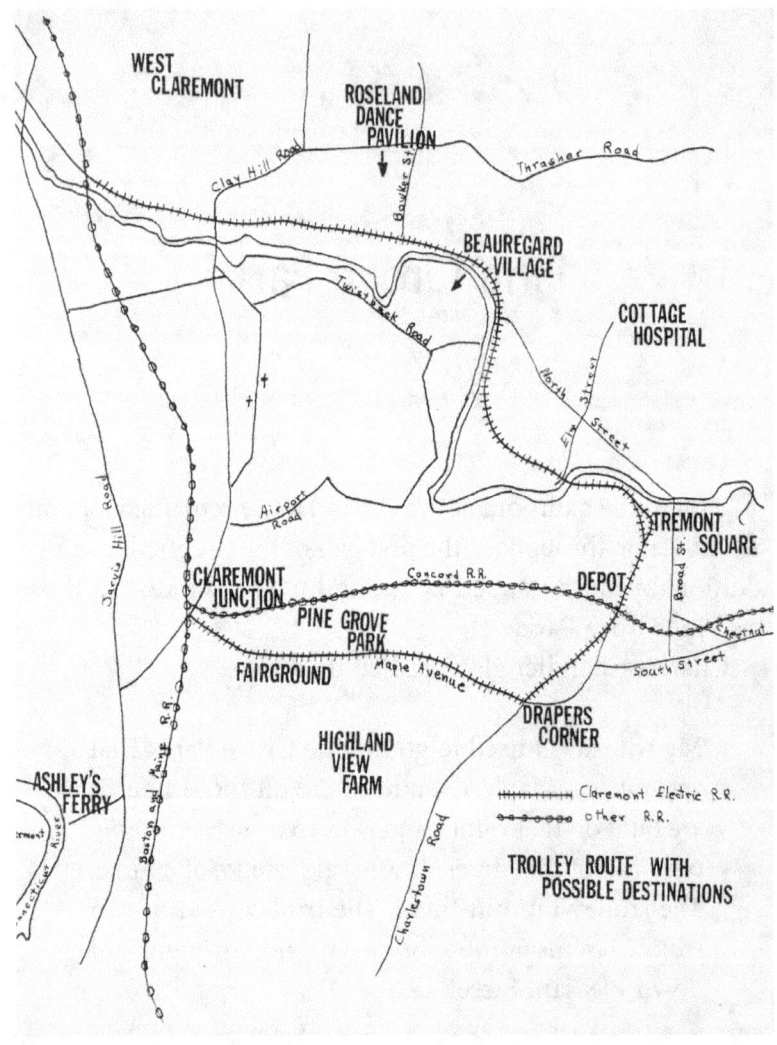

Trolley route possibly sketched by John Patch as part of his oral history. The tracks should have extended straight on Pleasant Street to Draper Corner, then turned right on Maple Avenue, instead of veering onto W Pleasant.

You'd dance in the dark and all these red, yellow spots and everything. And he got some of the best bands. Name the top bands and we had 'em here in Claremont. Surprising. You wouldn't think you'd have the same band you'd have in New York, but we did.

I first started going there in 1924.

Frank Bush also remembered Pine Grove Park:

> Barnes Park, Monadnock Park, and Moody Park had not arrived. On Maple Avenue was a private summer recreation area called Pine Grove Park. It also had a dance hall that featured one of the smoothest floors around.
>
> Automobiles were a rich man's toy then, so you either walked the two-mile distance, or for a nickel, you could ride the trolley car. Free dancing was offered in the afternoon.
>
> Many name bands played there such as Boutelle's of Massachusetts, and the great Duke Ellington Band from New York, and the Yale Collegians with Rudy Vallée, and local bands such as the Pine Grove Six, and the popular Frank Stone and his Violin. Then there was the snappy young band led by drummer Buster Keating.

Keating's Jazz Orchestra playing at Pine Grove Park in 1925

Rudy Vallée (1901-1986) was an American singer, actor, bandleader, and entertainer.

The Yale Whiffenpoofs are the oldest collegiate a cappella group in the United States, established in 1909. Best known for "The Whiffenpoof Song" a parody of Rudyard Kipling's Gentlemen Rankers, the group comprises college senior men who compete in the spring of their junior year for fourteen spots.

"The Whiffenpoof Song," the group's traditional closing number, was published in sheet music form in 1909. It became a hit first for Rudy Vallée in 1927 and later in 1947 for Bing Crosby. It has also been recorded by Elvis Presley, Count Basie, Perry Como, the Statler Brothers and countless others.

Excerpted from YouTube: Rudy Vallee - The Whiffenpoof Song 1927 Yale University

Pine Grove Park was not only for dancing, of course. Many types of events were held there, such as alumni events. Mable Cutting described her experiences at Pine Grove Park:

> Pine Grove Park was just woods. There was a dance hall there, and the orchestra would come for the summer. It was a Kavanaugh's Orchestra that used to come and stay all summer and play out there.
>
> When they had the alumni event in June, they would occasionally have it out there at the dance hall and would be catered by someone here in town. The girls got a dollar for waiting tables that night at the alumni event.

Pine Grove Park was also a popular location for picnics, including school and class picnics. Claremont resident Alice Joyal described St. Mary's School picnics at the park:

> Well, I went to [Pine Grove Park] when I went to school. We had picnics every year.
>
> They had the tramway to the park–to the junction. And our priest, Father Simard (pronounced See'-mahrd), used to attend to that. He used to see to it that on a certain day, after school ended, we had a picnic. And he hired the cars, I guess, the tramway. All the schoolchildren used to get in. And we used to sing going up there. That was a treat.
>
> We brought our own lunches. And they had booths there. If anybody had money, they could have bought different soft drinks or anything like that.

> We didn't have the money, but we had our lunches. Just a sandwich. And that was just the way we used to go down there. But it was nice.
>
> The school had games for the young ones. To pick up potatoes and run, and if you dropped the potatoes, you'd lose so much. We had quite a few things that kept us going all day. We used to play "lost my handkerchief," you know. The children together had to make a circle and we used to have a handkerchief and you could go around and around and drop it on someone else and if this one didn't catch it in time, the other one caught it. We used to have games like that.

The dance pavilion at Pine Grove Park burned down in July 1924.

Charles Chandler remembered this first fire:

> I remember one night we were out there on the 4th of July. It was intermission time. We were outside at the car, and someone says, "Look, dance hall's on fire. Good god."
>
> So, we left the girls at the car, and we rushed back in to get our jackets and coats we had, and came back out, and someone said to me, "Hey, grab a case of Coke or something." You know, trying to save what they could. So, I shoved a case of Coca Cola or something into my arms. And I took it out to the car.
>
> I didn't know where to take it. Everything was blazing, people were running all over. We got out of there. The

fire department took over, came out and got their hoses, all rigged up, out there on Maple Avenue. Some nut ran across the hoses and cut those in two. So, it was a madhouse. The whole place just burned down.

What happened was, they were dancing there and some wise guys are throwing firecrackers up underneath, and it was dry up underneath the floor. And it caught fire; all the band instruments, piano, everything went.

They had about three fires like that, and then they refused to insure it anymore. So that ended that.

Then they started one over here at Birch Grove over in Sunapee. That was quite a place, but my dancing days were over by then.

Claremont resident John Patch described some of the many events that happened at Pine Grove Park, and the first fire on the Fourth of July 1924:

They had ball games. They had picnics. Circuses. Carnivals.

They didn't have any cars in the park. The people that had cars were few and far between.

The streetcars had a track alongside the road. It ran alongside the road.

Pine Grove Park, it was big. It took up all of that side of Maple Avenue. I don't know how many

> acres, but it was big. Where all those houses are out in there, there was an enormous big dance hall, there was a grandstand, there was all kinds of booths out there. They had big ball games. They had Fourth of July.
>
> Fourth of July. That's when it burned. We were there when the dance pavilion burned.
>
> Somebody had thrown a firecracker underneath the dance hall. It was open underneath, you know?

Pine Grove Park was rebuilt, reopened, and burned down again in October 1926. Due to the multiple fires, the owner was unable to insure the establishment any longer, and Pine Grove Park closed.

After Pine Grove Park closed, the land was eventually subdivided and many of the houses built at that time along Maple Avenue still stand today.

Mable Cutting described the process:

> [Pine Grove Park] was sold off and gradually divided up into house lots out there.
>
> Of course, Moody Park was always an open spot there. Now it's for the city. It has built up a great deal out there on Maple Avenue.
>
> When I first went out, there were very few houses in back of Maple Avenue. Most everything was just on the avenue and there were mostly all larger houses. Then the small houses were built into that area.

Music Around Town;
Music at The Opera House

Music in Claremont in the Early Twentieth Century

For most, it's difficult to conceive a life not centered around the technology of computer, television, or radio, but life in the first decades of the twentieth century was devoid of those inventions. How, then, did people pass the time, especially on long winter evenings?

Albert D. Leahy Sr. describes a typical family evening in those days:

> The things we used to do together are gone. The olden days, you know, we used to sit around, a bunch of us. My father and mother and the neighbors would get around the piano Sunday nights. And then somebody would play and everybody would sing. And the whole family would all stay together. The kids would be there playing in the yard. You didn't have too many distractions. You didn't have nothing else to do. Now, so much is going on. You can't keep track of it.

Because sitting at home with family, creating one's own entertainment, was central to life at that time, many people learned to play an instrument. Therefore, a music store was essential to any town.

Paul Mason told of his father's music store and its impact on Claremont:

> My father had a music store in Bellows Falls, one of the early music stores. There was no television; there was no radio. It was just a music store.
>
> When I graduated in 1916, my folks were moving to Claremont when my father was putting in a music store here. My uncle ran the one in Bellows Falls, and my father ran the one up here and that's how I happened to come to Claremont.
>
> In those days, the music store business was greatly dependent on the several piano teachers in the area. And my accompanist Elinor Colby, who was a very brilliant pianist, was a piano teacher. They had reams and reams and reams of all this stuff for the kids, you know, as they came along from bracket to bracket in their ascendancy, in their musical career. Then they had instrumental music.
>
> And aside from that they had all types of sheet music. They had shelves on shelves of every conceivable kind of instrumental music, vocal music, all types of orchestra music.
>
> I myself, after I left prep school, studied voice in Boston for two years. I was a tenor soloist in

northern New England, probably one of the best, for thirty or forty years. And I worked at Joy along with it. I worked at Joy starting in 1916 and they let me go if I had a concert somewhere, if I had a church job somewhere, they'd let me go.

The big names, Rudy Vallée and Cab Calloway, they always came to my father's store when they came up here and made personal appearances. Of course, I was then probably seventeen or eighteen years old. I was the life of my friends because of who I associated with. "Why that guy, he knows Cab Calloway and his sister, and he knows Rudy Vallée." And this is a nice thing.

That's when Pine Grove Park was right at its height, they played out there, you know, a lot of the big bands. They made a regular procession of 'em going through there. This is around 1916, well into the twenties.

The piano business was very predominant in being an artist and being in the business. I had a Baldwin Grand [Piano], which I got from my father, the first thing when I went to work in the piano business, a tremendous thing in those days. Baldwins, Steinways and Chickerings—all the brands that we still have in the concert world, this was their heyday.

Music continued in the new local venues, such as Pine Grove Park and later Roseland, but the Claremont Opera

House remained a strong musical presence throughout this time. Paul Mason continued:

> Claremont was a very musical town. I sang in the Opera House several times. Most of my work was with the Vermont State Chorus. I was with them for five straight years. They had a big operatic chorus which the Women's Federation in Vermont ran. They got together once a year with a director from New York and put on a big concert.
>
> It was always something. It might be *The Creation*. It might be *Elijah*. It might be a Gilbert and Sullivan operetta. For five straight years, I had that job. While I was doing that, Maurice Longhurst whom everybody loved, and was one of the nicest guys in the world, had the music at Dartmouth. He did a couple of Gilbert and Sullivans; he did two or three of the light operas. And he always had us come up and do the solo work for him. It was really quite a thing.
>
> I've sung in probably fifty or seventy-five places, but the Opera House, I think it had the best acoustics of any place I've ever sung in.
>
> There wasn't a flat spot anywhere. Frequently you would find in the game I was in, that you'd have to go in for your pre-rehearsals and you'd find certain dead spots around on a stage of that size, where your tone didn't go out to the backseats.

My wife was a concert violinist. She was very versed in this sort of thing. She sat back in the back seat, and she spotted these things and told us when the things were coming through. But never at any time do I ever remember that we had a flat spot in the Opera House.

Between 1918 and 1919 and up through the forties, I was singing all the time. That was the most productive part of my life. I was the soloist in the Old South Church in Newport for twenty-five years.

I had a friend down in the Boston English Opera Company who was the lead tenor, and his name was Norman Arnold. He got the Boston Opera to come up and do Travatoria in the local opera house. This is one that everybody remembers because they built the tower where he sings his farewell song, probably forty feet high. It didn't look very solid to me. And Norman weighed about 275 pounds.

He had one of these gorgeous, great big, beautiful voices. And he was up there singing, and that tower was swaying. And my wife Gretchen and I were in the front seats, and I swore to God Norman was gonna be in our lap before that thing was over. But they got the curtain down, and the tower never came over.

That was one of the nicest things they've ever done here. People today speak of it. The older people remember the one time that the Boston English Opera Company came to Claremont.

The Opera House was really bustling. It was a constant thing. Throughout the year they had practically a steady flow of stuff, from say the late teens up through thirties and, and even up to the forties, it was a very, very active place.

We were all in that from time to time. We did a show called Broken Dishes. There was a man named Charlie Jobes in Newport, who was known all over New England for his musical and directing ability. He was a great friend of mine, and he came over as a personal favor to me and put on a show called Broken Dishes, which they asked to be repeated, and they repeated it two nights because people liked it so well.

SPOTLIGHT

Jazz, Swing and the Big Bands from New Orleans to Pine Grove Park and Roseland

The end of the 1920s brought a new form of music: jazz. Popular from the late 1920s through the 1940s, jazz and its big band spinoff, swing, made dancing popular.

This spotlight features Frank Bush's recounting of that time period in musical, and Claremont, history:

> Many books have been written on the origins of jazz. Consensus of opinion has it that its roots were in the city of New Orleans. However, little was known about it until 1917 when phonograph records brought it to the attention of the remaining parts of America and later to the world.
>
> In the late 1920s, jazz, which was also called Dixieland, had been unorganized—sort of

every man for himself—but in the 1930s and 40s, larger groups with choirs of saxophones and brass were being heard on radio, from coast to coast in swanky hotels and in ballrooms.

There were no superhighways, and automobile transportation was precarious and uncertain. Trolley cars were the popular way to get to an amusement park. Large dance halls and ballrooms came into being.

Claremont had Pine Grove Park and Roseland. This ushered in the big band era and was the first genuine mass music revolution in America. It was a coast-to-coast explosion of sound and songs and pop sensations.

The thirties and forties were a time when everyone who was young was a big band buff. One of the fabulous jazz trumpet players was Bunny Berrigan. He really never got started and died at the early age of thirty-three.

But we are getting ahead of our story. So, we take you back to the early 1900s in New Orleans where jazz is the only purely American art form. There are many opinions as to the origins of jazz. Most agree, however, that the roots of this art began some 300 years ago with the singing of spirituals and work songs of the African slaves being forced to labor in the broiling sun while shackled together in chain gangs. At night to rest their weary bodies, as they lay exhausted, it was customary for someone to strum a homemade banjo or guitar that was made from a discarded cheese box.

The blues gave a melancholy aura to the music, and when hearing them sung by the immortal Bessie Smith, the emotional impact was overwhelming.

As the slaves began to buy their freedom and drift toward the cities such as New Orleans and Memphis, musical instruments became more obtainable. The south became a cultural melting pot: French, Spanish, West Indians, Africans, all mixed together.

Small marching bands were formed to play for funerals, parties, and picnics. The most performed selection while escorting the body to its last resting place was

Just a Closer Walk with Thee. Happy in the thought that the soul had gone on to meet its maker, the musicians and mourners marched and danced back to town to the tune of *When the Saints Go Marching In.*

Up to this point in our pre-radio or -TV age, one had to learn a new song or musical composition by hearing it played on the parlor piano or by the town band.

Thomas Edison invented the phonograph, and everyone called it the talking machine. The first sounds emitted from the cylinder record and the morning-glory shaped horn sounded weak and scratchy. There were no microphones, and concert orchestras had to record through a series of horns. The year was 1917 and the phonograph changed the course of musical history.

The first recording bearing the name "jazz" was done in that year by the original Dixie Jazz Band, a group of white musicians that grew up in the South. The piece was *Tiger Rag* and is still in the repertoire of Dixieland-style bands.

The small bands of that time used no music. As most players could not read and depended on their native talent to produce what was labeled the Dixieland style.

In the 1920s musicians looking for lucrative work played for their bed and board on the Mississippi River boats and introduced happy music to Chicago and to New York and other Northern cities.

Within a short space of time, these small groups of musicians became known and accepted as Dixieland and jazz bands. At first, the spelling of the name was divided between J-A-S-S and J-A-Z-Z.

The listening and dancing public began accepting this new music, which in turn gave rise to many significant soloists, such as Sidney Bishay, and Bix Beiderbecke. However, one name dwarfed all others. He was a virtuoso jazz soloist who learned to play the trumpet in a New Orleans orphanage and became famous as America's Goodwill Ambassador. His name was Louis Armstrong, affectionately known as Satchmo.

Duke Ellington was born in 1899 in Washington, DC. In the 1920s, he formed a small band that played in dance halls throughout the East. In fact, he played in Claremont at Pine Grove Park, a popular place located off Maple Avenue, and the dancers had to arrive there by trolley car.

He arrived in New York as jazz was emerging from speakeasies. Radio broadcasting was then in its infancy. So, after receiving a sustaining radio program, his record sales soared, and he was on his way to fame.

His death in 1974 left a legacy of over a thousand songs, played all over the world for kings, queens, and other nobility. Duke's famous quote was "It don't mean a thing, if it ain't got that swing."

During the 1920s, the great [black] bands were still restricted from performing in the major hotels and dance palaces. Meanwhile, Paul Whiteman arrived from the West Coast surrounded with twenty-five or thirty musicians. He rearranged semi-classical music to be played in rhythm for dancing. He won the favor of the café-society people and was an instant success.

The phonograph record companies were hard-pressed to keep up with the demand he created, while Paul Whiteman was misnamed the King of Jazz.

More than any other single organization in the Depression years from 1929 into the early thirties, Glen Gray and his Casa Loma Orchestra helped us set the stage for specially arranged and organized jazz. This elegant-looking group of musicians brought to the public and college kids, an exciting mixture of big band jazz and slow sentimental ballads. It was matched by no other band of its day.

This moment also marked the beginning of electrical amplification and microphones. Their short trombone player had to stand on a chair as the mic stands were fixed and could not be raised or lowered.

On a historic night of August 21, 1935, Benny Goodman, his clarinet and his band playing their theme song *Let's Dance* opened on the West Coast and the

Palomar Ballroom, which was the world's largest. They were a screaming success.

They enjoyed an extended stay, then returned to New York. Here, they received a warm welcome at the Paramount Theater. After the ten-minute long *Sing Sing Sing* featuring not only Benny's clarinet, but Harry James's trumpet and Gene Krupa's drumming, swing was born.

Big bands that came to Roseland, starting with Isham Jones, playing *Stardust* and then the Dorsey brothers: Tommy with his trombone, with his vocalist, Frank Sinatra, and his brother Jimmy playing alto saxophone.

There was Artie Shaw and his clarinet. Near the end of the swing era, one band overshadowed all others in its appeal to the public. Even today, it is the most remembered sound of the thirties and forties: Glenn Miller and his orchestra.

In World War II, Glenn Miller joined the army.

Rudy Vallée with his megaphone and orchestra came. And *The Post* reported that the attendance at his dances broke all records.

Harry James, with the blessing of his former boss, Benny Goodman, started a swinging band that played all over the country until his death in 1983. Frank Sinatra got his [true] start as a vocalist in the band.

From Kansas City came the hottest band to set the dances jumping. It was led by a great pianist Bill Basie, and they called him the Count.

Cab Calloway became a great band leader who did not play any instrument.

In the thirties and forties, a band led by Woody Herman called the Band that Plays the Blues. Woody has kept a band together for 40 years, and it has won its second Grammy Award.

The late Stan Kenton Band was born during the upheaval of the World War II years. Its debut was made in the Balboa ballroom in Southern California. Both Stan and Woody helped to keep the big band movement alive through the fifties and sixties.

The late 1940s saw emphasis switched from the big bands to the small groups. It was first called Bee Bop and later shortened to Bop. Dizzy Gillespie and Charlie Parker were the early proponents of this type of music.

For over 40 years, the nation first listened to radio, and then watched on TV, the late Guy Lombardo and his band play the old year out, and the new year in, from the Waldorf Astoria in New York.

Lawrence Welk, who was a Dakota farm boy, began pleasing the dancing public with his Hotsy Totsy Boys back in 1925. Through the medium of television, he has had the most successful band in America. He recently retired and is enjoying a weekly program of his musical memory.

The Paulette Sisters were born in Claremont. They were taught the art of singing in showbiz by their mother. While they were still in their teens, their parents brought them to New

York where, after winning several amateur radio contests, they recorded with Connie Boswell and Larry Clinton.

In 1937, the Yacht Club Orchestra reorganized as a cooperative group. Soon, Ted Allen joined as pianist and arranger. During World War II, the younger members were called upon to serve Uncle Sam. They played in service bands and upon their return home, they rejoined the group.

The June 1983 issue of Yankee Magazine has a picture of a wedding at Hildene featuring The Bob Cunniff Big Band.[1]

---

1   Hildene is Robert Lincoln's home in Manchester, VT.

ROSELAND: A New Type of Music; a New Venue

After Pine Grove Park burned down and closed for good, a new music and dance venue, Roseland, opened in Claremont, just as jazz and big band swing was rising to popularity. Frank Bush, who frequently played there, described it:

> A new one called Roseland was opened in West Claremont. Nationally famous bands play there on Thursdays. The Yacht Club Orchestra, a local band, played there on Saturday nights. The featured vocalist was Frank Cleary.
>
> I can't say too much about it, except that it's just like any dance hall. It was started in 1927 after Pine Grove Park burned down. For a few years, it was operated only on Saturdays and Thursdays.
>
> Perhaps the first year or so, they ran three nights a week, but it was a boom thing for a year or two. And then it changed hands and began to lose out

because of lack of transportation to get out there during the war, and of course the Depression, too.

So they went through the Depression, and then you had the problem of during the war: the traveling bands, most of the boys were in the service. They were not the good bands that we'd had before. After the war, then they started coming back.

So, Roseland had to weather a lot of different problems. The last fellow who had it winterized it. And of course, that helped to keep it going, until the days the big dance halls were done.

Yacht Club Orchestra performs at Roseland ~ 1947

What was it about Claremont that drew big names to its dance venues? Frank Bush also described the geographical logistics of the time:

> We were probably the largest town in the area, just like the shows. We were geographically situated in that we were halfway between Boston and Montreal or Burlington. Claremont made a good high halfway place because traveling in those days was not as easy. You didn't have your throughways or expressways, and cars were not that good. So, if a band left Boston in the morning, it would take them all day to get to Claremont, adding all the problems that might have with tires, that type of thing, and the roads.
>
> The bands would arrive here in time to stay overnight, so they might as well. Being that there was a dance hall, they might as well book here and play. They'd either have a sleeper bus, or some bands, they had the sleeping bags, and they'd sleep on the dance floor at night. The next morning they'd head off from here to go to Burlington or Portland, Maine where there was another big dance hall.
>
> We were close enough to Dartmouth College to attract the students down here. There was no dance hall that large in Lebanon or Hanover or White River.

Roseland

Bertha Emond remembered her limited experience observing Roseland from the outside:

> I don't remember Pine Grove much except riding on the open car to get out there once. I was very young, but Roseland I used to love. I both danced and roller skated out there. But my mother wouldn't let me, when I was still at home—I lived at home until I got married—but I didn't go dancing there much because my mother wouldn't allow me.
>
> I was very protected, overprotected, and she wouldn't let me go out. I don't think it had a reputation. It may have had. My mother protected me so much, she wouldn't have told me even. She just wouldn't let me go.
> But we used to drive out when the big bands came and sit out and listen to them and you could get over to the screens and look in, you know, you

could stand outside and look in and see them. But they always kept it so dark, it was hard to see the dancers, but that's all I remember.

Earl Bourdon remembered Roseland from his childhood:

I can remember when I was a young boy who only had to walk a couple hundred yards up to the Roseland dance hall, when it was built. It was built when I was ten years old. And I can remember going up there like everybody else in Claremont did to hear the Dorsey brothers, to hear Paul Whiteman, to hear Cab Calloway and Duke Ellington.

Roseland burned down in 1950 and was later torn down.

Band Music in Claremont

In the first half of the twentieth century, the burgeoning demand for live music—from movie theaters to dance halls and beyond—made many a professional career. Claremont had its first Stevens High School band in those days.

Stevens High School band 1924-25 with Buster Keating as drummer

Frank Bush explained how it came to be:

> I got my start in music while I was in school because our principal was Albert Kellogg and Albert Kellogg had retired from World War I. He was a captain or a major in the army and he always had a flair.
>
> He played some musical instruments himself. He had been teaching before Claremont in Manchester. He started the first high school band in Manchester. High school bands were a novelty back then; there weren't very many. He came to Claremont, and he said we ought to have one here.
>
> And so, he sent out a word for people and our music teacher was Dan Ladd, who was a violinist and hated band, but he had to do it. So, we organized the very first band Stevens ever had in my senior year.
>
> I always wanted to play the saxophone, but I couldn't afford one. So, I managed to pick up a secondhand trombone for $12. So, I was a trombone player, and we had a lot of fun. We practiced all winter long. Finally, we got good enough to march down through the square, into Monadnock Park for the opening of baseball season.
>
> That was my beginning in music.

As technology advanced, and the Victrola yielded to phonographs, more families were able to listen to recorded music in their homes. Mr. Bush recalled how residents attained music, especially remembering the significance of the Masons' music store:

> Records probably were the thing that people would listen to, to hear dance bands and dance orchestras. We didn't hear symphony on records too much at first. They began to come out later, but there would be singers like Caruso, some of the famous Italian singers would be on Victor records, which I can remember. We used to buy a record a week from Mason's Music Store, which was the music store in Claremont.
>
> It was on Pleasant Street, right next door to Powers Shoe Company. He was the Victor agent. Of course, he sold pianos. Every home had a piano, no television, no radio. You had to make your own music.
>
> So, as we began to hear Paul White on records, that whetted my appetite, I suppose, and the saxophone was a new instrument.
>
> Of course, I was sort of discouraged; the musicians in Claremont were either playing in the orchestra pits or were playing in the marching or the American Band, which gave concerts every Thursday night.
>
> And for dancing, they would come over from the bandstand. After the concert, which wouldn't be over till 10, they'd come over to the Town Hall and play for dancing until midnight.

One of the famous songs was *Dardanella*. They probably played three times that night, but there were no saxophones in the band. Once in a while, an orchestra would be engaged from Dartmouth College and they'd come down, they'd have all the new instruments, such as saxophones and banjos, which no one played around here.

They'd played just legitimate instruments, like flutes, trumpets, trombone, that type of thing. So, of course that whetted my appetite even more. I wanted a saxophone.

Finally, I was able to pick up a banjo, and I started playing a few chords and all of a sudden, I'm in great demand. All the orchestras in Claremont then realized that if they were going to compete with these out-of-town orchestras from Boston or from Dartmouth, they had to have either one or the other, a banjo or a saxophone, or they wouldn't get hired.

So, I was playing with everybody, and getting on the job training, in other words. And there were no books to teach you how to play the banjo. You had to just more or less play by ear. But this violinist Frank Stone had an orchestra, and he would take his violin, and play the four notes of the chord on his violin, and I found them on the banjo. That's how it got started. I was reading music for my trombone lessons, but that didn't help me on the banjo. I still kept my trombone going. And finally, one day I bought a saxophone and I had three instruments. And from there I kept going that way.

> Dardanella is a 1919 song with music by Felix Bernard and Johnny S. Black. It was published by Fred Fisher, who also wrote the lyrics. Band conductor Ben Selvin recorded the song with his orchestra, making it a hit recording. (Jordan)

Eventually, Bush became a professional musician, who toured and performed on radio:

> I was working at the Army-Navy on the corner of Tremont Street and Tremont Square (now called Opera House Square) and they would allow me to play on Saturday nights, to get out to play with different orchestras.
>
> And finally, after about a year, I was offered an opportunity to play with an orchestra from Gardner, Massachusetts. They were playing at a summer resort. Those were big things like we had in Claremont, Pine Grove Park, etc. We played in Concord, New Hampshire, an amusement park and played in Fitchburg, and then Gardner.
>
> A buddy of mine from Claremont, his name was Lee Loveland, had gotten a saxophone. He had been a clarinet player and he was very good.
>
> He went to college, but he dropped out of college just to play. We were both playing with Boutelle's.

So, he had an opportunity to go with the Paul Whiteman unit called the SS Leviathan Orchestra; it was the big transatlantic liner at the time. And they had a band on the ship, and they had gotten off the ship and they were making tours and he had this opportunity to join them.

Through his contacts, I learned of an orchestra in Worcester, MA. They were going to start broadcasting. It was just the very beginning of broadcasting.

So, I joined Benny Resh. And this was a very nice group. We used to play a restaurant three times a day. And they had this restaurant, which was a department store restaurant that owned and installed this radio station, which is today, WTAG at Worcester. And so, we were broadcasting live because records were still not good enough to be played [on the radio].

As you know, today, they were 78s and they were scratchy.

We traveled to Florida for a season, New York for a season, the Great Lakes for a season. I decided to come back to Claremont and to have a family, by this time. I guess I got sick of traveling around.

After touring as a professional musician, Bush returned to Claremont, and taught music in the region at a time when school music programs were expanding:

I had learned while I was away that the public schools were beginning to want music taught, instrumental music, where they originally would have only a vocal group, that type of thing, or an orchestra for graduation, and that was it.

I went to Sunday schools, to the University of Michigan, then international music camp at Interlocken. This was just the beginning of World War II. School bands were coming in big; the old town bands were sort of petering out.

I came back, and one time I was doing instrumental music in five schools, one each and every day of the week: Charlestown, Chester, Claremont, Lebanon, and White River Junction.

I knew I couldn't keep everything going. So, I whittled down to three bigger schools, but I gave up all the schools, but Chester, Vermont. I stayed there sixteen years, retired from there, 'cause it only took one day a week.

SPOTLIGHT

Buster Keating Local Music Celebrity

FROM RAY KEATING'S "BUSTER KEATING: BANDLEADER"
In the days of jazz and swing, one of the most well-known names in the Claremont music scene was Buster Keating. Buster, and his wife, Anna eventually owned a home on Crescent Lake, and was remembered by his son, Ray, in this feature article from the Crescent Lake Association's website.

Buster Keating was born in 1906. He displayed a talent for music at an early age.

His mother, a former schoolteacher, saw to it that he studied piano, classical guitar, and drums. He played in the Stevens High School band and in the orchestra. He also joined the American Band and a local symphony orchestra.

When the Magnet Theatre was built, he was employed to play there for silent movies. Following the construction of the Latchis Theatre on Pleasant Street he played with local musicians in the pit orchestra.

The orchestra, led by Frank Stone, a classically trained violinist from Claremont, played during silent films and as accompaniment for various vaudeville acts.

In the summer of 1924, he traveled with Frank and other Claremont musicians, Frank Bush, Frank Stone, and Art Burgess, on a tour of the grand hotels of New Hampshire's north country.

Buster formed his first band "Keating's Jazz Orchestra" during his junior year at Stevens High School. A talented musician, he was also a natural self-promoter. His band became very popular at the time and was featured at high school proms and receptions in Claremont, Bradford, and Lebanon, NH, Windsor, and Bellows Falls, VT, and other nearby towns.

Buster formed his first band Keating's Jazz Orchestra during his junior year at Stevens High School.

Travel at that time was somewhat limited to railroad trains that served the area. The original band was composed of local musicians, but after graduation in 1925, several of the original members left town to attend college or take jobs in other towns. They were replaced by musicians from Claremont and Newport, as well as Springfield, Woodstock, and Windsor, VT.

Upon graduation from high school, Keating decided to pursue a career as a professional musician and ran various bands and jazz orchestras for more than twenty years.

In the early 20th century nearly every town had at least one dance hall. Claremont's first outdoor ballroom was located at Pine Grove Park on Maple Avenue. For those who just wanted to listen to the music, 10 cents got them on the grounds outside the pavilion.

Three months out of high school, Keating's was the featured band on Saturday nights at Pine Grove Park. As the band began to travel to out-of-town dance halls and clubs more often, Buster purchased a nine-passenger Peerless touring car to accommodate the band members and their instruments.

The band played one night stands in northern New England and southern Quebec, staying in inns and lodging houses while on the road.

This was the time of Prohibition, and it was not uncommon for the band to encounter roadblocks set up to intercept smugglers bringing liquor down from Canada, where it was legal. These checkpoints were frequently manned by soldiers with machine guns and Tommy guns. Stories were told of band members crossing the Canadian border with pints of whiskey taped to their ankles beneath their bell-bottom trousers.

After signing with Paul Sullivan, the top booking office for New England and Canada, the band experienced great popularity throughout the area. In 1926 he signed a contract with the Lake Sunapee Yacht Club to be the house orchestra during the summer seasons.

Taking the name, The Yacht Club Orchestra, the band played at the Yacht Club until well into the 1940s.

In 1929 he went to New York City and auditioned for, and was awarded, a contract with the United Fruit Company's White Fleet to play on one of their cruise ships. Before the contract could be executed, however, the Roaring Twenties ended with the collapse of the stock market and the beginning of The Great Depression. The contract was canceled, and the cruise ships never left the harbor.

To make ends meet, Keating took a day job in the accounting department of Loft Candies on Long Island, New York, one of the largest candy makers of the day. However, he continued searching for music opportunities.

At that time, he contacted a good friend and former Claremonter, Joe Joy, a top-flight orchestra leader and in charge of recording at RCA Victor Records. With his help and contacts, he met New York musicians and the door was opened for him.

He played in studio bands backing up recording sessions for major jazz stars and played at the Arthur Blyth Dance Studio. He canvassed the music publishing offices on Broadway and Tin Pan Alley.

One way to get work was to go to the musician's union hiring halls for artist calls. He was hired by the Myer Davis Orchestra, a society orchestra, to play with a fourteen-piece orchestra at the Caroline Country Club in White Plains, NY when he was first introduced to the big band sound.

Around this time, he contracted a serious case of strep throat, and was unable to work. Anna, his soon-to-be wife, went to New York City and brought him back to Claremont to nurse him back to health. While he still wanted to pursue a career in music, he decided to get married and stay in Claremont, and the ongoing Depression persuaded him to enter a new career.

He sold insurance for a couple of years, then bought out a small insurance agency. He and Anna moved into his parent's home on Trinity Street, and he began selling insurance from home.

He reactivated the Yacht Club Orchestra, focusing on summer jobs at the Lake Sunapee Yacht Club and became the house orchestra for the newly built Roseland Ballroom in Claremont.

The band also became popular for high school proms. During the Second World War, many members of the band were drafted, requiring a rebuilding of the orchestra.

Dancing and listening to big band music were very helpful in keeping morale up, and the band was very much in demand at Roseland and other dance halls. The band adopted uniforms which resembled US Navy uniforms and many stages were decorated with military motifs.

Going to the Saturday night dance at Roseland was a major social event for many Claremonters. With so many men gone for the duration, many wives came alone to the dances, and it was not uncommon to see women dancing with each other. The dance floor was usually crowded for every dance.

When the Yacht Club Orchestra was the featured band, there would come a moment when the dancers would begin to shout, "Bus-ter, An-na, Bus-ter, An-na." This would be the cue for Buster to leave the stage and dance with Anna.

The crowd would clear a large space in the center of the floor to make room for them to dance. After they did a few turns, the other dancers would applaud them and return to the floor to finish the dance with them.

Springfield, and Windsor, Vermont were heavily involved in defense contracting during the war.

Morale boosting concerts were held on the factory floors.

With the end of the war, the demand for big band music began to diminish, and many organizations were forced to disband. Buster struggled to keep the Yacht Club Orchestra going as long as he could, but in 1947 he decided to retire from the music business.

Buster quit the music business and devoted his full time to growing his highly successful insurance business. For a while other members of the band tried to keep the organization going, but with little success.

As big bands disappeared and dance halls were closed down (or in many cases burned down), many local musicians were forced to find full-time employment in other industries. Yet their love for the music led them to form small groups of four to six musicians to play together when they weren't working at their day jobs.

These groups were usually formed by a talented trumpeter, piano player, or other soloist who would then enlist a mix of other musicians who played the instruments that would round out the band's sound. Typical groups would consist of piano, drums and bass for backup, and one or two brass or reed players. Other bands would feature a vocalist.

During much of the 1900s membership in a club was a major part of a community's social life. There were the fraternal orders such as the Elks, Moose, and Masons, and there were ethnic clubs like the Polish/American Club, Italian/American Club or whatever other ethnic groups had enough members to start a club.

There were also veteran's clubs like the American Legion and the Veterans of Foreign Wars. In addition, there were many bars and nightclubs in the surrounding communities. Many of these clubs and bars had dance floors and would hire these smaller bands to entertain their members on Friday or Saturday nights. Thus, the music was kept alive.

Other musicians, who didn't belong to a band or were not working on a particular night, would often visit these clubs and bars to listen to their fellow musicians perform. It was quite common for members of the band to call up these musicians to sit in with the band on a few numbers throughout the evening.

If the guest musician played a brass or reed instrument, they usually carried it around with them and were always willing to augment the group. Piano players, drummers, and bass violin players were always willing to hand over their instrument to the guest and take a short break.

For many years after the Yacht Club Orchestra was disbanded, younger musicians, many of whom had done time with Buster's bands, would call him up to the bandstand to sit in on a number or two. Everyone knew Buster Keating, and, to these young musicians, he was an icon.

As the popularity of this form of music grew, many clubs began to run charity concerts that were billed as jam sessions, where several of the local bands would take part. Each would play a set, and then listen to the other groups do the same. These events would occur on a Sunday afternoon, and usually went on for hours.

Many of the musicians would be called up to sit in with the other bands or to showcase a particular talent. Proceeds from ticket sales and drinks would be donated to the club's favorite charity. As an incentive to the musicians to participate they were usually admitted free and were given free or discounted drinks from the bar. Most of these musical groups played the new jazz form that had evolved from the big band sound into less structured music in which the musicians often improvised around the theme of popular dance music.

There were some groups that specialized in the music of specific ethnic groups. While the Polish/American Club in Claremont usually featured this form of jazz, the Polish Grange in Claremont's Lower Village featured Al Godek's Polka Band.

As the older musicians retired from music or died, the popular music culture turned more and more toward rock and roll. Slowly the little jazz groups started to dissolve until, by the late 1980s, they had all but vanished. However, many of these old-time musicians continued to be drawn together to reminisce about the good old days and play a few tunes to show that they still had it.

VII. Other Entertainments and Local Parks

Other Entertainments and Local Parks

Of course, movies and music were popular and successful forms of entertainment in the early twentieth century, but they were not the only ones. Claremont had its fair share of sporting events, and even circuses.

Other than the sports played at the Town Hall, there were many parks throughout town which featured amateur and semi-professional sporting events. Albert D. Leahy Sr. remembered baseball in Claremont:

> We had a team years ago, the Claremont Braves, in 1914.
>
> But then, the Claremont Pilots were a semi-pro team. There were a group of us, all sponsored. And the Pilots had the New York Yankees who could furnish us with two players. Each big-league team could furnish one of the Northern League Players with two players.

In those days the kids had to go to ball games. So, they had their uniforms and had pictures taken with them.

We had Claremont, Bennington, Glens Falls (New York), Burlington, and St. Albans; and it was good. It was a good league.

It was popular in Claremont and we'd get good crowds. We used to play at night at Monadnock.

But that year—that was in 1940; Pearl Harbor was in 1941—that September I went to New York to hire a fellow to manage the team, a new team. He got all set practically and then Pearl Harbor came, and that was the end of that. A lot of those folks were killed in the war.

Speaking of parks, when I was a kid, I used to have Sunset Park up on Broad Street. There was a twilight league, a merchants' league.

There was a field, Cossitt Field, and that was a baseball park. There was a grandstand there, and they used to have the twilight league there.

Across from where the middle school is now, on the other side of the tracks, down where a lot of houses are now, is this little street that goes down off of Broad. That was Sunset Park.

And they'd have baseball teams and football teams. That used to be a pretty good league too.

Everybody in town had a team, Monadnock Mills had a team, the shoe shop had a team. They all had teams. We played at night, and it was good. We used to get good crowds.

Pine Grove Park is often remembered for its dance hall. However, its expansive grounds also contained several ball fields and was a site for many sporting events. Leahy also remembered:

> They used to play out to Pine Grove Park; they had a ball field out there.
>
> That's off Maple Avenue where, you know, where you see Rose Avenue, that used to be a park. There used to be a dance hall and a park.
>
> And I remember they had a game there against Newport. Murphy, who lived in Newport, he was great. He'd hire all these fellows.
>
> Major League Baseball Player, Jumping Joe Dugan, who played for the Boston Red Sox and the New York Yankees—among other major league teams—had two brothers, Leo and Lynn that played for Holy Cross in the outfield. They played for Newport this summer. They were good ball players.
>
> Murphy hired the Dugans, but they didn't do any work. A lot of our players were college players. And so, there was some restriction on what they could do, but theoretically, they had jobs, but practically they didn't work. Theoretically they were washing cars here.

Jumping Joe Dugan

They got good pay and they didn't work.

You could only pay a manager in those days a thousand dollars a year to manage. But there was such a thing as fringe benefits. I know one manager we had, he could go up to a gasoline pump and pump his gas, and nobody would charge him anything. Of course, all these merchants were part of the deal running the league.

We had good games and good ball players. Of course, times have changed. You don't have those things now. You couldn't get people to go out.

Leahy also remembers events in Barnes Park, including when the famous Buffalo Bill Wild West show came to town:

> We had the 101 Ranch, Buffalo Bill, also known as William F Cody, come up here. He had Jess Willard, American world heavyweight boxing champion, with him. Jess Willard fought Jack Dempsey and lost his title to Dempsey on July 4, 1919. Jess Willard was the main attraction. We all had to go, and they put on quite a show.
>
> Of course, the big thing in those days was the circus parade. That was a big thing, 'cause all the Native Americans would be on their horses, coming down and the cowboys would be there. Boy, the kids would get a kick out of those "Cowboys and Indians."
>
> Those were the things we had to enjoy. We didn't have any television or radio or things like that.
>
> Anytime you had an occasion, you had a parade, 'cause that was a big deal in the old days, to parade. And they always had parades.
>
> And they had field days, a lot of field days going, everybody went to, and those are the things that you enjoy. They had all kinds of games for kids to play, blind men, three-legged races and all sorts of games. Folks would sit around. They'd have games and fun and eat.

VIII. The End of The Opera House?

Another Big Shift in Entertainment Pushed the Opera House into Near Obscurity

As radio, and then television, became commonplace in homes, there was a shift in live entertainment which impacted many entertainment venues in Claremont, and most especially the Claremont Opera House.

When asked when the Opera House began to go downhill, Frank Bush recalled:

> I'd say between the fifties and sixties; it was never used, hardly. The city didn't seem to be interested in keeping the roof from leaking and various things.
>
> I think after World War II, we began to dwindle down. When Claremont went from a town to a city, there was no more need for town meetings, which used to always be held in the Opera House.

In 1930, Stevens High built a large gym, and they had their own graduations. That was the end of graduations at the Opera House.

So various things began to happen. Then the armories were built for dances or larger events than the hall downstairs could accommodate, and also the city needed the rooms for offices. So they just began to forget the place upstairs; let it go.

There were no more traveling shows after the late twenties.

The Claremont Lions Club minstrel show in the 1950s

With no traveling shows brought in for entertainment, the Opera House served as a venue for local entertainment primarily:

> There were no more shows coming through just local shows put on by the steel workers, the Rotary Club, Penny Sales, something like that.
>
> The Rotary Revels were just a home talent show, a minstrel show. You'd hire someone to come in and put it on. Once in a while, there'd be a local person who could do it.
>
> The need for the Opera House and so forth was over. I mean, for prized road shows, there were no more, they didn't travel.
>
> That was pretty much true throughout the United States.
>
> The Claremont Lions Club sponsored a minstrel show in the 1950s. For several years, the Rotary Club would present a review. It was called the Rotary Revels, and all proceeds were directed to local charities. Perhaps the last minstrel show was put on by the Claremont Steel Workers in 1962.

Bertha Emond, whose husband Charles Emond was Claremont Opera House stage manager from the 1940s to the 1960s, recalled the 1960s at the Opera House:

> It was mostly hometown things that I remember there. I think people stopped vaudeville further

back and they didn't travel with shows the way they used to.

The Rotary Club used to put on an annual event; the American Legion used to put on one.

The local organizations used to use the Opera House for various things.

With so little happening at the Opera House, around 1960 the downstairs ballroom was turned into office space and a city council chamber.

Because of the lack of use, the doors at the Opera House were closed a few years later. The city even contemplated removing the auditorium in favor of a more modern building for the city offices and the District Court.

It seemed the Opera House would disappear from the Claremont scene forever.

A Second Wind

But all was not lost for the Claremont Opera House. Claremont resident and then-Mayor Marion Phillips was instrumental in the effort to preserve and re-open the Claremont Opera House.

Cynthia McKee recalled Phillips' involvement in this effort:

> Marion Phillips was very active in the dramatic club and a very dear friend of mine all my life. I think I first got acquainted with her at the dramatic club, and we were talking about the Opera House.
>
> In fact, long before anything was done, she and I had talked about the possibility of getting it fixed up, so it would be usable again. At that time, she had a mayor's advisory committee.
>
> We did try to stimulate some interest in the Opera House. We didn't get very far because we were limited to using local people to come in and take a look at it to see if they thought it was feasible. Almost without exception, the men that we got to

go in said, "Oh, what do you want to fix this old place up for?" They showed no interest at all.

We did get some people to come down from the Hopkins Center at Dartmouth College.

So, by the early sixties it was finished.

Marion Phillips always felt that the reason it went downhill was that the auditorium was built at the high school. It was smaller, it was new, and everybody wanted to use it.

Even the dramatic club started using it. The auditorium at the high school has no dressing rooms or anything like that. But for some reason the Opera House seemed to start to go downhill very shortly after that auditorium became available.

Things still did go on there, but no care was taken of it. So finally, it was just shut up.

But, as far as I was concerned, the stage at the high school was so far from being adequate. And the people we had who came down from Hopkins Center said that was a marvelous stage, that you just don't find them like that anymore. It's something about the pitch. I don't know enough about it. They were so impressed with the old scenery and with the acoustics.

In the sixties, people's attitudes were just "Forget the Opera House" or "Junk it."

There were even some people who talked about taking that upper floor off city hall, because the Opera House was just sitting there, not being taken care of and deteriorating to a certain extent. And I suppose they thought that they could make the whole building more efficient if they took it off. I guess that was a thought. I don't even remember who suggested it now, but I remember hearing it and being so horrified.

The city began taking the space in the Town Hall for city offices in the late fifties, early sixties.

I felt bad, especially about the glass doors on the front of the building.

I suppose Marion probably did more for Claremont than any other woman in my lifetime. She worked very hard. She was interested in a great many things. As I said, she was interested in dramatics. I think she was a teacher by education.

She was a Councilwoman for a great many years and finally mayor for a great many years. I thought she was almost the ideal woman politician.

She worked very hard for what she believed in, and she wasn't defeated easily. With the Opera House, when we tried to get something started, I guess we both knew it wasn't going anywhere. And she said, "Well, it just isn't the time to do it."

She would've tried again, but unfortunately, she became very ill before that happened.

Philips did succeed in preventing the Claremont Opera House from being razed and turned into office space. It was boarded up until the time was right. The campaign for preservation and reopening of the Opera House eventually did take hold.

A Restoration Committee was formed in 1972. The Restoration Committee completed the application for the building to be placed on the National Register of Historic Places, with the help of Cynthia McKee, featured in these pages. George Gilman, State Commissioner, assessed the application and nominated it on behalf of the State.

According to the Claremont Opera House website:

> Through its efforts, the Opera House was placed on the National Register of Historic Places in 1973 and funds were raised to hire an architect by 1975.
>
> With the joint effort of the City Council and the Opera House Restoration Committee, a NH Historic Preservation Grant was received for a feasibility study in 1976.
>
> In 1977, the Restoration Committee became a non-profit organization, Claremont Opera House, Inc. With plans and studies completed, the city applied for and received a grant from the Federal Economic Development Administration. The municipal complex became a reality. Interior restoration was funded by a federal grant from Heritage

Conservation and Recreation Service, Claremont Opera House, Inc., and friends.

The Claremont Opera House also received a Comprehensive Employment Training Act Grant to cover staffing to plan the reopening.

Frank Bush recalled the reopening performances and celebration:

> In 1977, the Opera House committee met with city, state, and government officials in the dusty old orchestra pit to discuss the long road ahead for complete rehabilitation of the old Opera House.
>
> On Saturday, May 26th, 1979, the Opera House opened to a near full house of over 800. The orchestra director was the talented David Strohmeyer. There were many fine voices in the cast, including Marlene Hartley as Rosalinda, and Marilyn Stearns as Adele, and Ted Blaisdell as Alfred.
>
> The orchestra, comprised of semi-professional musicians, local students, and music teachers was unusually good and its sensitive accompaniment to the soloist proved Sanders to be a well-disciplined conductor.
>
> The new atrium glowed like a giant lantern at night, and they also added a new self-service elevator to all floors.

Since the grand reopening of the Opera House on May 26, 1979, the Friends and Boards of Directors have raised funds, both publicly and privately, to re-equip the house. They have expanded programming and hired a director with the vision of once again becoming the entertainment center of the area.

IX. Claremont's Cultural Future

Claremont's Cultural Future

The Claremont Opera House has long stood as a symbol of hope—of what could be in a place which has always had industry and hard work at its core.

Earl Bourdon put it this way:

> I think the whole attempt to renovate downtown Claremont, the concept behind the renovation of the Opera House, the whole inducement of the concepts that result in both of them is an attempt to make it possible for Claremont to offer more in terms of the cultural, the intellectual, and the arts.
>
> One thing I like best about Claremont is the fact that there's a community awareness in an organized, directed fashion with some planning that Claremont should have a role and should have a future—and that role and future should include the whole concept of beautifying the inner city and providing some hope for cultural activity and intellectual activity in the community.

> This whole renovation of the Opera House is an idea that's pregnant with possibilities, not only for more arts and crafts and more music and more lecture programs, but I think it's a symbol of the effort of the community to revitalize the nature of life in Claremont.
>
> I think that an appreciation of the arts in its broadest sense: music, lectures, plays, skits, anything else enriches the lives of people, because it gives you broad horizons of the whole question of living.
>
> I think this whole concept of change in Claremont: the beautification of the city, the development of that—the arts, the development of a broad range of cultural activities—will be an inducement, not only to keep more of the young here, but to attract more of the people who have ideas. I think it's a great thing.

The Opera House stands as a symbol of a community with a solid foundation, but which reaches high with new ambitions. As noted in the application for the historical register:

> These ambitions are only now becoming attainable, through renewed commitment to the community by its citizens – a commitment sparked by recognition of the quality and potential value of its heritage and natural resources. (1973)

Yet, *The National Eagle* said it best, in its 1897 article lauding the Opera House's construction and presence in this community:

Providing no accident happens, [The Opera House] will remain our public building for many years to come, and the *Eagle* trusts and predicts that it will serve the purpose well, and that as time passes everyone will have increased pride in the noble structure, than which there is no finer in any town in New Hampshire. Solid, substantial, made upon honor, beautifully finished and decorated, and with every modern appliance. We can go there for our public gatherings, and take visiting friends there on gala occasions, and feel that Claremont has got as good as the best in the public building line.

Afterword

In November 2021, when Kit Hawkins and I were introduced to *Claremont, New Hampshire - A Living History* at the Fiske Free Library, we knew we needed to bring this oral history back to life. 2022 is the 125th anniversary of Claremont's "public building" that houses city hall and the opera house, and we wanted to celebrate this historical milestone. We formed a 125th anniversary committee and applied for a NH Humanities grant to fund a writer.

This book was published as a result of a six-month committee effort between participants from the City of Claremont, Fiske Free Library, Claremont Historical Society, Off Broad Street Players and the Claremont Opera House (COH). The project will also result in the creation of other historical and cultural events in the years to come.

Over the last 125 years, thousands of events were held within the Claremont Opera House and City Hall, while others were held at the many theaters, dance pavilions and parks around the city. A personal goal for this book was to remind Claremont's long-time residents, and to educate recent residents, about our very special past. It is a past filled with music, theater, culture, sports and intellectual pursuits. It is a past also filled with debate and differences of opinion about support for the arts and capital investment in the arts.

The Claremont Opera House has been through phases of success and failures over the decades, leading to its closure in the early 1960s. It then reopened in 1979 with a capital campaign that funded a massive restoration in the early 1980s, returning the theater to its original state with the addition of the atrium gallery and an elevator. Since then numerous capital improvements were made through efforts of the Board of Directors.

Today, the maintenance of this grand dame theater is still plagued with capital investment challenges and declining community support. Membership dwindled from a high of over two hundred donors twenty years ago, to a low of only thirty-five in 2019. At the start of 2020, the Board set a goal to renew community support but COVID soon followed, creating new challenges for a renaissance of the theater. Thankfully, a combination of grants and of support from our long-time donors enabled the COH to survive through 2020-21, and plan expanded programming for the future. We hope past audiences and supporters will return in 2022.

This book roughly covers a period from 1895 through to 1980. The 125th Anniversary Committee is planning to capture the last fifty years of progress through another living history to be recorded by our partner at Claremont Community Television. Through this effort, you will hear more stories about the decades since the COH reopening.

The restoration of the Claremont Opera House - City Hall and the revitalization of the downtown core forty years ago, is repeated this year with the City investment in Pleasant Street, the development of the Claremont Creative Center and the ongoing capital improvement planning of the City Hall Complex. It was Earl Bourdon who said it best in his

1980 interview: "This whole renovation of the Opera House is an idea that's pregnant with possibilities, not only for more arts and crafts and more music and more lecture programs, but I think **it's a symbol of the effort of the community to revitalize the nature of life in Claremont**."

Residents who did revitalize the nature of cultural life in Claremont included Addison Wyman, Harry Eaton, Paul Mason, Bill and Frank Bush, Charlie Emond, Mildred LaPanne, Marion Phillips, Cynthia McKee and many others. Who will we write about in the future? I know Claremont's current advocates for the arts include Ed Evensen, John Bennett, David Putnam, Sharon Wood, Melissa Richmond, Shelly Hudson, and John Lambert. What will their story be for our 150th Anniversary in 2047, and who else will we add to this list? Only time will tell…

Felicia Brych Dalke
Board President, Claremont Opera House

Works Cited

1908 Lyman H. Howe Travel Films ~ movie Flyer. Vintage Movie Ads. (n.d.). , from www.atticpaper.com/proddetail.php?prod=1908-lyman-h-howe-movie-handbill. Accessed 23 Mar. 2022.

"Albert Dennis Leahy Obituary." *The Eagle Times* [Claremont, NH], 2 Mar. 1994.

"Bertha Rita (Vernette) Emond Obituary *The Eagle Times* [Claremont, NH], 17 June 1991.

Bourdon, Phillip L. "Family Folklore or Just Tall Tales?" *The Eagle Times*, Eagle Printing & Publishing LLC, 16 July 2019, www.eagletimes.com/features/family-folklore-or-just-tall-tales/article_79f43360-6885-5a4e-aac9-29d85e1e1541.html.

"Charles Frederick Chandler Obituary." *The Eagle Times* [Claremont, NH], 31 Mar. 1995.

Clifton-Waite, Paul. "Activist 'Lion,' Bourdon Succumbs to Cancer at 75. " *The Eagle Times* [Claremont, NH], 21 June 1993, p. 1.

Croft, G. "A Living History: Claremont Oral History Completed." *Valley News*, 25 Oct. 1980, p. 9.

"Cynthia Lestine (Weed) McKee Obituary." *The Eagle Times* [Claremont, NH], 13 Sept. 1994.

"Dance Pavilion at Pine Grove Park Is Destroyed by Flames." *Claremont Daily Eagle*, 5 July 1924, p. 1.

"Dedication Number." *The Claremont Advocate*, 23 June 1897.

"Earl Murray Bourdon Obituary." *The Eagle Times* [Claremont, NH], 21 June 1993.

"Effie Hazel (Ladeau) White Obituary." *The Eagle Times* [Claremont, NH], 12 Mar. 1992.

"Elizabeth M. Bell Obituary." *The Eagle Times* [Claremont, NH], 24 Dec. 1989.

Emond, B. "Gift of Oral History." *The Eagle Times* [Claremont, NH], 22 Oct. 1980.

Emond, Bertha. "Claremont Oral History." Interview Tape 5, by G. Gatz, 7 May 1980.

"Frank Walter Bush Obituary." *The Eagle Times* [Claremont, NH], 14 May 1996.

Gatz, G. (1980, April 24). Claremont Oral History: Interview of Earl Bourdon Tape 1. personal interview.

Gatz, G. (1980, May 6). Claremont Oral History: Interview of Alice Joyal. personal interview.

Gatz, G. (1980, May 7). Claremont Oral History: Interview of Bertha Emond Tape 5. personal interview.

Gatz, G. (1980, June 11). Claremont Oral History: Interview of Arthur Garneau. personal interview.

Gatz, G. (1980, June 16). Claremont Oral History: Interview Mildred LaPanne. personal interview.

Gatz, G. (1980, June 19). Claremont Oral History: Interview of Charles Chandler Tape 20. personal interview.

Gatz, G. (1980, June 25). Claremont Oral History: Interview of Mable Goodhue Cutting Tape 22. personal interview.

Gatz, G. (1980, June 30). Claremont Oral History: Interview of John Patch. personal interview.

Gatz, G. (1980, July 8). Claremont Oral History: Interview of Effie White Tape 21. personal interview.

Gatz, G. (1980, July 16). Claremont Oral History: Interview of Cynthia McKee Tape 33. personal interview.

Gatz, G. (1980, July 18). Claremont Oral History: Interview of Albert Leahy Tape 44. personal interview.

Gatz, G. (1980, August 4). Claremont Oral History: Interview of Paul Mason Tape 31. personal interview.

Gatz, G. (1980, August 4). Claremont Oral History: Interview of Cynthia McKee Tape 34. personal interview.

Gatz, G. (1980, August 15). Claremont Oral History: Interview of Elizabeth Bell Tape 40. personal interview.

Gatz, G. (nd. 1980). Claremont Oral History: Interview of Frank Bush Tape 37. personal interview.

Gilman, G. "National Historical Register." Concord, NH, 26 Apr. 1973.

Hawley, Samuel. "The Birth of the Feature Film – 120 Years Ago: The Corbett-Fitzsimmons Fight (1897)." Bright Lights Film Journal, 28 Mar. 2017, brightlightsfilm.com/birth-feature-film-120-years-ago-corbett-fitzsimmons-fight-1897/.

"History." *Claremont Opera House*, Claremont Opera House Board of Directors, https://www.claremontoperahouse.info/history/. Accessed 10 Mar. 2022

Jordan, Nathaniel. "Dardanella - Ben Selvin (1919)." YouTube, Google, 15 Feb. 2013, www.youtube.com/watch?v=7NBUqd-wI-Us. Accessed 12 Mar. 2022.

Joyal, Alice, "Claremont Oral History." Personal Interview by G. Gatz, 6 May 1980.

Keating, Ray. "Buster Keating Bandleader." www.crescentlakeassn.org, Crescent Lake Association, www.crescentlakeassn.org/history/pdf/Buster%20Keating%20&%20Yacht%20Club%20Orch.pdf. Accessed 12 Mar. 2022.

"Mable Edith (Goodhue) Cutting Obituary." *The Eagle Times* [Claremont, NH], 24 July 1998.

"Many Make Merry at Reopening of Park." Claremont Daily Eagle, 8 Aug. 1924, p. 1.

Naqi, Sheza. "The End of an Era: From Silent Film to Talkies." *ETEC540: Text, Technologies – Community Weblog*, University of British Columbia, 28 Oct. 2012, blogs.ubc.ca/etec540sept12/2012/10/28/the-end-of-an-era-from-silent-film-to-talkies/. Accessed 23 Mar. 2022.

"National Register of Historic Places." *National Parks Service*, U.S. Department of the Interior, www.nps.gov/subjects/nationalregister/index.htm. Accessed 20 Mar. 2022.

"Paul Ole Mason Obituary." *The Eagle Times* [Claremont, NH], 3 Sept. 1989.

"Pine Grove Dance Pavilion Fire Swept." Springfield Reporter, 28 Oct. 1926, p. 8.

"Pine Grove Park to Reopen this Evening." Claremont Daily Eagle, 7 Aug. 1924, p. 1.

Sterling, Christopher H, and Robert Curley. "*Radio*." Encyclopædia Britannica, Encyclopædia Britannica, Inc., 29 Sept. 2011, http://www.britannica.com/topic/radio.

The Claremont Advocate (Claremont, N.H.) 1881-1941." *The Library of Congress*, lccn.loc.gov/sn84020388. Accessed 20 Mar. 2022.

"Thomas Winston (Buster) Keating Obituary." *The Eagle Times* [Claremont, NH], 30 May 2001.

Town Hall Dedicated: Interesting Ceremonies in Connection with the New Building." *The National Eagle*, 26 June 1897, p. 5.

"Vitaphone." *George A. Smathers Libraries*, University of Florida, www.uflib.ufl.edu/spec/belknap/exhibit2002/vitaphone.htm. Accessed 23 Mar. 2022. Wancho, Joseph. "Joe Dugan." *Society for American Baseball Research [SABR]*, 17 Sept. 2012, sabr.org/bioproj/person/joe-dugan/.

warholsoup100. "Rudy Vallee - The Whiffenpoof Song 1927 Yale University." *YouTube*, Google, 27 Apr. 2011, www.youtube.com/watch?v=ODnaBjjgfgA. Accessed 20 Mar. 2022.

Board President's Acknowledgements

Writing and publishing a book is a demanding process when there is a single author, let alone when a book is created through the efforts of many people and organizations. Balancing project priorities from different perspectives can become impossible without tradeoffs between schedule, cost, content and quality that can change as the project progresses. Our different perspectives have come together to produce this book, with tradeoffs, that will educate our community for generations to come.

First I want to acknowledge the financial support from New Hampshire Humanities (NHH) that not only funded the writing of this 2022 book, but also funded the original 1980 oral history project on which this book is based. Thank you Gerald Gatz for leading the 1980 project and sharing your memories with the project team. Thank you Agnes Burt and Catherine Winters for your current NHH support.

This book would not be possible without the research assistance from the Fiske Free Library and the Claremont Historical Society. They introduced the 1980 oral history to us and contributed historic content from many sources. Both organizations held the bar high when it came to ensuring we produce an accurate history. I have made tradeoffs at times but I hope the final product will come close to meeting their high standards.

As the book was being developed, committee members from Off Broad Street Players suggested possible spin-off projects. They will use the stories preserved here to create living history performances and adapted scripts that we hope will entertain and educate audiences for years to come. Thank you Trudee Bacon, Kara Lee, and Sharon Wood. I particularly want to thank Sharon for her partnership and dedication, and for leading the effort to capture "Claremont, NH - A Living History, Part Two".

A heart-felt thank you to David and Cindy Putnam, and Andre Lafreniere from Claremont Custom Framing and Art Restoration for donating their time to capture and enhance most of the images contained in the book. We are privileged to have David's creative mind involved. Also, many thanks to Josh Nelson and Claremont Community Television for partnering with Sharon to capture new oral histories about arts and entertainment from the last 50 years.

Many thanks to Edward Evensen and Raymond Keating for sharing their scrapbooks and stories about the big band era in Claremont almost a hundred years ago.

To Christine (Kit) Hawkins, Stephanie Harris, Nancy Meyer and the other board members from the Claremont Opera House: thank you for your input and guidance on this project, for putting up with my proposals from left field, and for trusting me to take financial risks on a book. Thank you to Kit for creating a 125th Anniversary Exhibit, and to Joella Merchant for participating on the 125th Committee. To Andrew Pinard, the COH Executive Director, thank you for your patience as we focused on this book, for producing the 125th Anniversary show, and for your help as we launch the book with spinoff efforts. Lastly, my sincere appreciation to John Bennett for his dedication to the COH since the 1970s, and for sharing his vast knowledge of COH history.

Many thanks to Claremont Savings Bank for their financial support of the book production process. They are a long time advocate for the COH.

Finally, thank you to Annalisa Parent, the writer and publisher. We are fortunate to have you involved in this project, not just as a contracted publisher, but as someone with deep roots in the community and fond memories of the Claremont Opera House. It is your commitment to this project that has helped us navigate the tradeoffs and get the book across the finish line. We all thank you!

List of members of Claremont Opera House 125th Anniversary Committee

Trudee Bacon, Off Broad Street Players
Felicia Brych Dalke, Claremont Opera House
Stephanie Harris, Claremont Opera House
Christine Hawkins, Claremont Opera House
Kara Lee, Off Broad Street Players
Joella Merchant, Claremont Volunteer
Nancy Meyer, City of Claremont and Claremont Opera House
Sharon Wood, Claremont Historical Society and Off Broad Street Players
As well as others from the Fiske Free Library and Claremont Historical Society

Author's Note

As a sixth-generation Claremont resident, writing this book was a special undertaking for me. I'd grown up with my grandmother reminiscing about her days dancing at Roseland, and personally attending Joy's Annual Christmas Party at the Opera House. As a young child watching Woody Woodpecker films or laughing at magical acts on its stage, I had no idea that the venue had only just reopened. Yet, even as a child, the majesty of the Claremont Opera House did not escape me.

The Claremont Opera House is a treasure to this community. What I have discovered culling the archives of our rich cultural history has invigorated me for a bright future, a renaissance of sorts, wherein multiple venues offer varying types of entertainment for residents to enjoy.

It is my ardent hope that in these pages you have found a connection to this place, to its beauty, and to its heritage that will inspire you in some meaningful way, too.

Author's Acknowledgments

This book would not have been possible without the Claremont Opera House 125th Anniversary Committee. *Stage Whispers: A Living History, Retold*—a brilliant title they devised—is only a small part of the larger effort they've organized for this momentous occasion for such an important place. They spent tireless hours culling audio material to select the narrators featured here, and offered their input on the direction of this piece every step of the way.

Felicia Brych Dalke has directed an effort with nearly countless moving parts with inspiration and grace. She was always there to answer a question, clarify the direction, or effuse enthusiastically about all the history we'd uncovered.

Fact checkers Felicia Brych Dalke and Sharon Wood kept this work on the straight and narrow by ensuring the narratives and research were correct.

On my own team, Mary Joy Dinampo and Caylie Porter helped with transcriptions and excerpts. Without their help, I'd still be hunting and pecking away at the keyboard.

Special thanks to Bob Cunniff for meeting me for coffee to talk about Frank Bush and big band music.

About the Author

Annalisa Parent helps writers to finish, publish, and sell their books. She is the CEO of Laurel Elite Books, a two-time teacher of the year nominee, and a recipient of the French congressional Medal of Honor for a peace-promoting speaking tour of France, in French.

Annalisa writes for many local, national, and international publications, has written and produced sketches for a Telly-Award winning CBS television show. She and her work have been featured on Huffington Post Live and PBS, and in the *New York Times* and Associated Press, as well as many podcasts, radio and television programs.

Her book *Storytelling for Pantsers: How to Outline and Revise your Novel without an Outline* is a recipient of a CIPA EVVY Silver award for Best Business Book, and a finalist in the humor category. She was a long-time journalist for South Burlington, Vermont's *The Other Paper*, and a member of the White House Press Pool.

She has ghost written many books and projects including transforming audio files into book form for Dreamscape Media; and writing the Community Health Needs Assessment and Population Health Plan for the Vermont Department of Health.

Annalisa has taught writing around the world, spoken at writing conferences in New York, London, Paris, Boston, and beyond. She has taught writing and literature at Norwich University on the undergraduate and graduate level, as well as at the Colorado Writing School.

When she's not writing, you can find her walking her dog in Moody Park, camping with her Girl Scout troop, or volunteering with the Claremont-Sugar River Rotary Club.

Sponsorships

This commemorative book would not be possible without the support from these organizations.

NEW HAMPSHIRE
humanities

www.ingramcontent.com/pod-product-compliance
Lightning Source LLC
Chambersburg PA
CBHW050352120526
44590CB00015B/1666